Kingfisher first dictionary

CW01663608

KINGFISHER

KINGFISHER

First published 2005 by Kingfisher
an imprint of Macmillan Children's Books
a division of Macmillan Publisher's Limited
20 New Wharf Road, London N1 9RR
Basingstoke and Oxford
Associated companies throughout the world
www.panmacmillan.com

ISBN 978-0-7534-3287-7

Copyright © Macmillan Children's Books 2005

All rights reserved. No part of this publication may be reproduced, stored in or introduced into a retrieval system, or transmitted, in any form or by any means (electronic, mechanical, photocopying, recording or otherwise), without prior written permission of the publisher. Any person who does any unauthorized act in relation to this publication may be liable to criminal prosecution and civil claims for damages.

2 4 6 8 9 10 7 5 3 1
1TF/0211/WKT/RNB/PICA/105MA

A CIP catalogue record for this book is available from the British Library.

Printed in China

This book is sold subject to the condition that it shall not, by any way of trade or otherwise be lent, resold, hired out, or otherwise circulated without the publisher's prior consent in any form of binding or cover other than that in which it is published and without a similar condition including this condition being imposed on the subsequent purchaser.

Cartoon illustrations: Rachel Conner (Linda Rogers Associates)
Photography: Tim Ridley, Nick Goodall

About this dictionary

Grolier First Children's Dictionary has been specially written and illustrated for children who are learning to read. The words in the dictionary have been carefully selected from those which young children see and use every day. As well as being easy to use and fun to browse through, this dictionary will help children develop the skills that will enable them to become confident users of more adult dictionaries. Younger children will enjoy looking at the colourful pictures and matching them with the words; older children will have fun consulting the dictionary for meanings and spellings.

This dictionary has a number of key features which combine to make it an indispensable learning tool:

▷ **Definitions** are carefully written in clear, simple English. **Example sentences** show how to use many of the words, and the attractive **illustrations** and **photographs** help to clarify the meaning of words.

Simple **spelling tips** alert children to words that sound the same, and help to guide them to the place in the dictionary where they will find the word they are looking for.

▷ The bright **picture pages** on topics such as shapes, animals and cars will reinforce the meaning and spelling of familiar words and broaden the young reader's vocabulary.

▷ **Word play** boxes encourage the child to make active use of the dictionary in order to solve a variety of word games and puzzles, so developing important word skills and building confidence with using a dictionary.

Occasional **Word origin** boxes provide a first entertaining insight into the way certain words have come about.

▷ The **Spellchecker** lists many of the commonest little words in the language. These are the words which are not likely to be looked up for meaning, but some of them may be difficult to spell.

Contents

Using your dictionary

b c **d** e f g

The **letter string** on every page helps you to remember the order of the alphabet and to find the word you are looking for more quickly.

Pictures and photographs help you to understand the meanings of words.

If a word has more than one meaning, each meaning has a number before it.

Here you can see how to use the word in a sentence.

note
1 A **note** is a short letter to somebody. The **note** says Sarah has gone swimming.
2 A **note** is also one sound in music.

goose (geese)

For some words, there is a special way of talking about more than one of the thing, so we say one **goose** but two **geese** (not two **gooses**). These special words are shown in the dictionary.

The dictionary also tells you how to say words that have difficult spellings.

rough *say *ruff*

geese Look at **goose**.

If you look up **geese** in the dictionary, it tells you that you need to look at **goose** to find the word explained.

This dictionary shows you the special ways of writing a word that tell you about when something happened:

Emma is **drinking** a glass of water now.

Emma **drank** three glasses of water this morning.

drink (drinking, drank, drunk)

Emma has **drunk** a lot of water today!

Some words change their spelling when they are used in different ways: I have a **big** present, Joe's is **bigger** and Mia's is the **biggest**. The dictionary lists these spellings.

big (bigger, biggest)

above

Above means higher than something. Your nose is **above** your mouth.

accident

An **accident** is something bad that happens which nobody has planned.

Amy's dad had a car **accident**.

ache

An **ache** is a pain in your body that goes on hurting, like **earache**.

acorn

An **acorn** is the nut that grows on an oak tree.

acrobat

An **acrobat** is a person who can do difficult and clever balancing tricks.

across

Across means from one side to the other. There is a bridge **across** the river.

act (acting, acted)

If you **act** in a play, you take part in it. Aziz **acted** in the school play. A person who **acts** is an **actor**.

add (adding, added)

If you **add** numbers, you put them together.

If you **add** three and two, you get five.

address (addresses)

Your **address** is the number or name of the building where you live and the name of the street and town where it is.

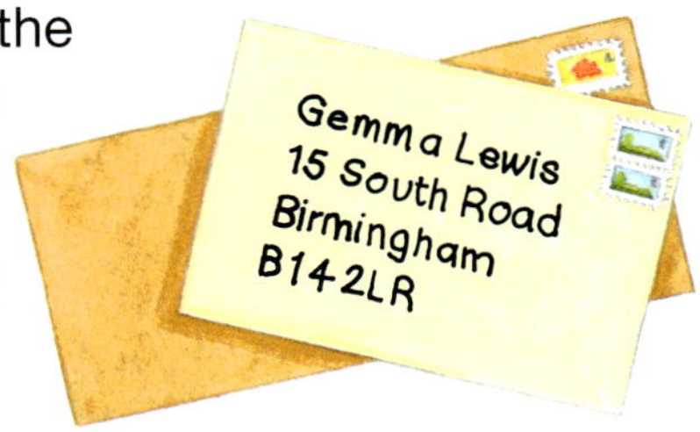

adult

An **adult** is a grown-up. When children grow up they become **adults**.

adventure

An **adventure** is an exciting or dangerous thing that happens to you. I am reading a book about the **adventures** of three children who got lost in the jungle.

aeroplane

Aeroplane means the same as **plane**.

afford

If you can **afford** something, you have enough money to buy it. Can you **afford** to buy your brother a present?

afraid

If you are **afraid**, you think something nasty will happen to you.

Are you **afraid** of spiders?

after

After means at a later time. I am going to my friend's house **after** school.

afternoon

The **afternoon** is the part of the day between morning and evening. We come home from school at half past three in the **afternoon**.

again

Again means once more. Sing that song **again**.

age

Your **age** is the number of years you have lived. Your **age** changes every time you have a birthday. Richard and his friends are all different **ages**.

agree (agreeing, agreed)

If you **agree** with somebody, you think the same about something. My sister thinks this is a good book but I don't **agree** with her.

air

We breathe **air**. It is all around us, and birds and aircraft fly in it.

aircraft (aircraft)

An **aircraft** is any machine that flies. Helicopters, gliders and aeroplanes are **aircraft**. (Look at the next page.)

airport

An **airport** is a place where aircraft take off and land.

alike

If two people or things are **alike**, they are the same in some way. Amy and Becky look **alike** because they are twins.

alive

A person, an animal or a plant that is **alive** is living now. Plants must have water to stay **alive**.

all

All means every one or every part of something.
All the puppies are brown.

alligator

An **alligator** is an animal with sharp teeth and a long tail. It lives in rivers in some hot countries. **Alligators** are reptiles.

allow (allowing, allowed)

When somebody **allows** you to do something, they let you do it. My dad sometimes **allows** me to use his computer.

Word play
How many words can the ape make by adding one letter at a time to the beginning of **all**?

Answers on page 176.

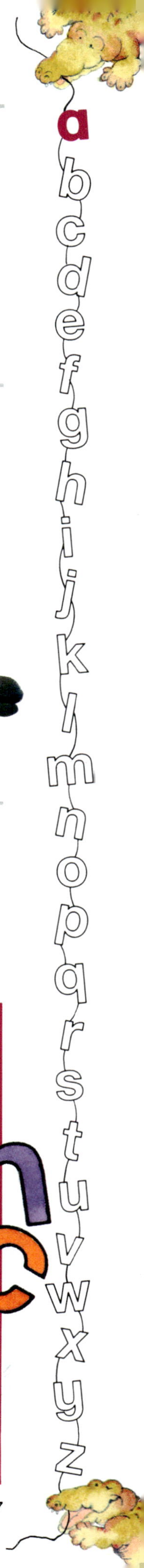

Aircraft

△ **Light aircraft** have **propellers** which spin round and round to move the plane forwards.

△ A **helicopter** has spinning **rotor blades** instead of wings.

▽ A **glider** is a plane without an engine.

△ A **passenger jet**

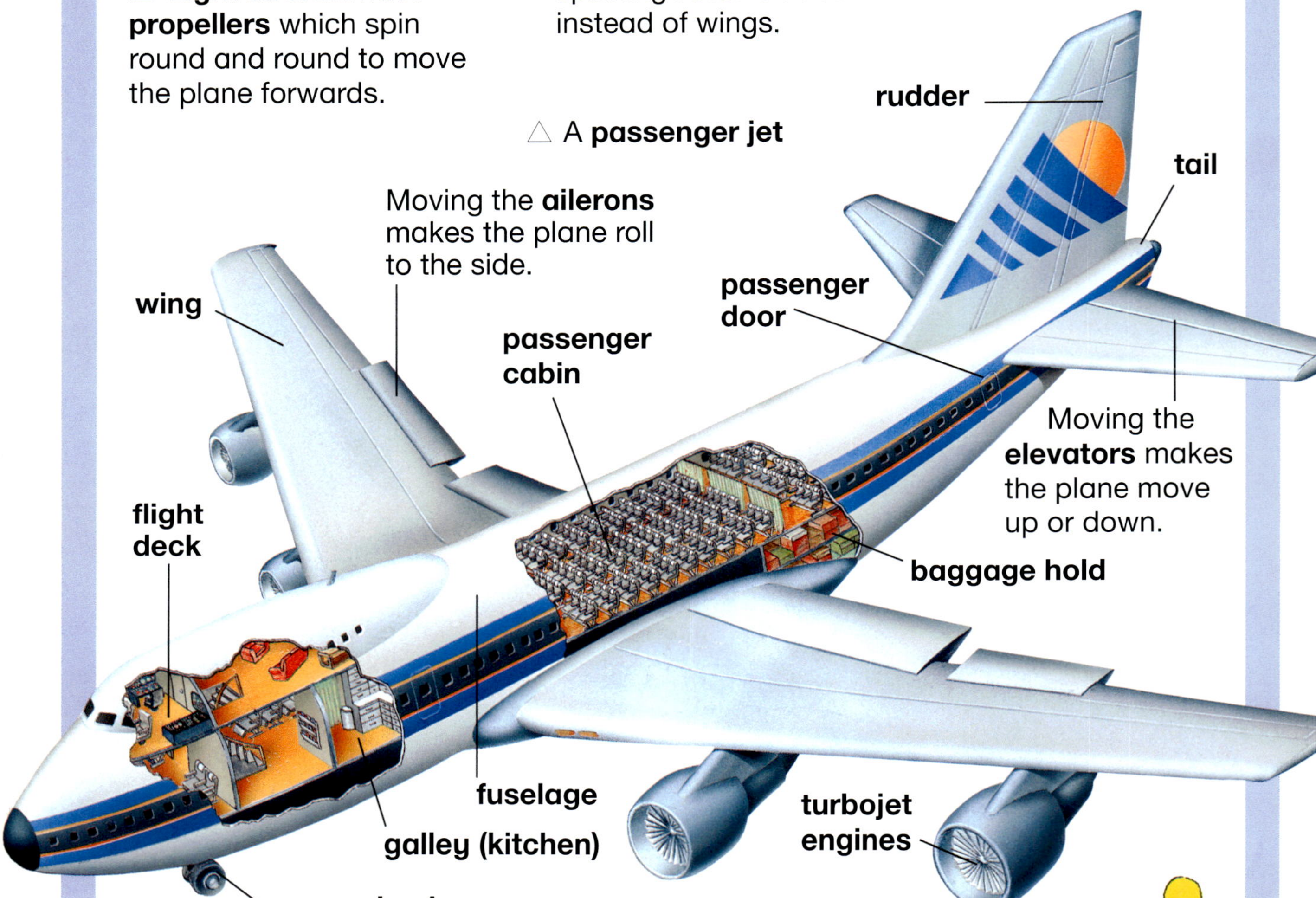

How do wings work?
To see how a plane's wings work, blow hard over the top of a piece of thin paper. The paper will rise up.

almost

Almost means nearly, or not quite. Ned can **almost** touch his toes.

alone

When you are **alone**, you are not with anybody else. I like to be **alone** when I am reading.

along

Along means from one end of something to the other end. There are trees **along** the river bank.

aloud

Aloud means not silently. Read your poem **aloud** so everybody can hear.

Another word that sounds like **aloud** is **allowed**.

alphabet

The **alphabet** is all the letters that we use to write words, from A to Z.

You can see the **alphabet** at the side of this page.

Alpha and **beta** are the first two letters of the Greek alphabet. Put together, they make the word **alphabet**.

always

Always means all the time or every time. It is **always** dark at night. I **always** go to bed before my brother.

ambulance

An **ambulance** is a large car or van for taking people who are ill or hurt to hospital.

amount

An **amount** of something is how much there is. I get the same **amount** of pocket money as my sister.

amphibian

Amphibians are animals that can live on land and in water. Frogs and toads are **amphibians**.

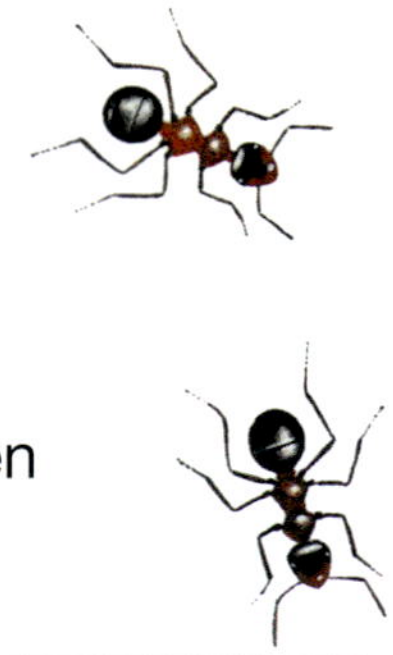

angry (angrier, angriest)

If somebody is **angry**, they are very cross. Dad was **angry** when my brother broke the window.

animal

An **animal** is anything that is living and can move around. Cats, whales, bees and fish are **animals**, but trees are not.

ankle

Your **ankle** is the part of your leg where it joins your foot.

annoy (annoying, annoyed)

If you **annoy** somebody, you make them angry. Ella is **annoyed** with me because I am late.

another

Another means one more. May I have **another** piece of paper?

answer

1 (answering, answered) When you **answer**, you speak to somebody who has called you or asked you a question.
2 An **answer** is what you say when somebody asks you a question.

ant

An **ant** is a tiny insect. **Ants** live in nests under the ground.

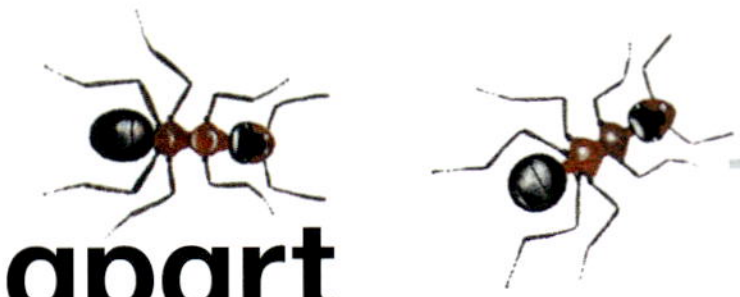

apart

1 Apart means away from each other. Stand with your legs **apart**.
2 If you take something **apart**, it is in pieces. John took the lamp **apart** to see if he could fix it.

ape

An **ape** is an animal like a big monkey without a tail. Gorillas are **apes**.

apologize (apologizing, apologized)

When you **apologize**, you say you are sorry about something that you have done.

appear (appearing, appeared)

When something **appears**, you can suddenly see it. The Sun **appeared** from behind a cloud.

apple

An **apple** is a round fruit with a green, red or yellow skin. **Apples** grow on trees.

Animals

A **toucan** is a **bird**.

A **beetle** is an **insect**.

A **goldfish** is a **fish**.

A **rabbit** is a **mammal**.

A **toad** is an **amphibian**.

A **turtle** is a **reptile**.

Some other groups of animals

molluscs

spiders

crustaceans

insect **bird** **amphibian** **mammal** **fish** **reptile**

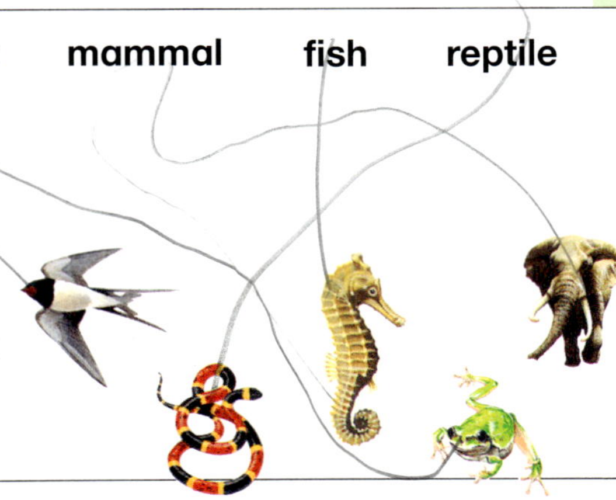

Animal groups
Do you know what these animals are called? Which groups do they belong to?
Answers on page 176.

area

An **area** is a part of a country or a place. We don't live in this **area**.

argue (arguing, argued)

If you **argue** with somebody, you talk in an angry way because you do not agree about something.

arm

Your **arms** are the parts of your body between your hands and your shoulders.

armour

Armour is a strong metal covering that soldiers used to wear to protect their bodies.

army (armies)

An **army** is a large group of soldiers who fight together.

around

Around means on all sides of something. There is a fence **around** the field.

arrive (arriving, arrived)

If you **arrive** somewhere, you get there. What time does the train **arrive**?

arrow

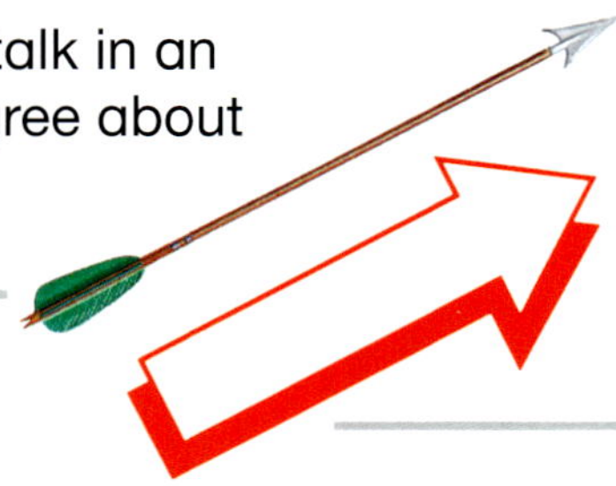

1 An **arrow** is a thin stick with a point at one end. You shoot **arrows** with a bow.
2 An **arrow** is also a sign that points to tell you the way.

art

Art is something beautiful that somebody has made, like a painting or a statue.

artist

An **artist** is a person who draws or paints pictures or makes other beautiful things.

ask (asking, asked)

1 When you **ask** a question, you are trying to get an answer. "Where is the nearest post office?" she **asked**.
2 When you **ask** for something, you say that you would like it. I **asked** for a drink.

asleep

When you are **asleep**, you are sleeping. Katie is **asleep**.

astronaut

Astronaut is made from two Greek words that mean 'star' and 'sailor'. So an astronaut is somebody who sails towards the stars!

An **astronaut** is a person who travels in space.

ate Look at **eat**.

atlas
(atlases)

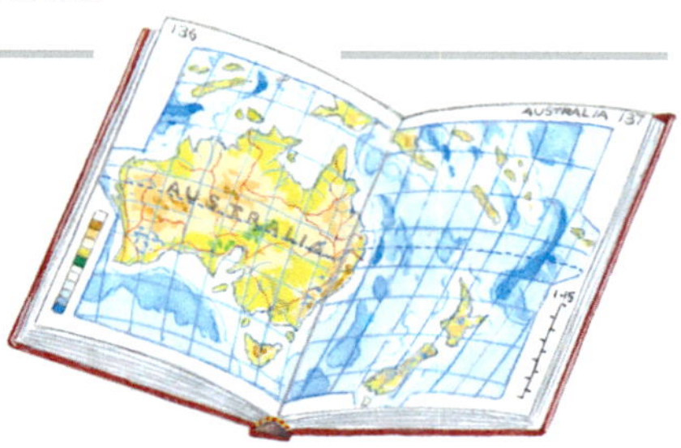

An **atlas** is a book of maps.

attack (attacking, attacked)

If somebody **attacks** another person, they try to hurt them.

attract (attracting, attracted)

When something **attracts** people or things, it makes them come closer.

audience

An **audience** is a group of people watching or listening to something like a play or film.

aunt

Your **aunt** is the sister of your father or your mother, or the wife of your uncle.

automatic

If a machine is **automatic**, it can do things on its own without being looked after.

autumn

Autumn is the part of the year that comes after summer. Leaves fall off the trees in **autumn**.

awake

When you are **awake**, you are not asleep. Katie is still in bed but she is **awake**.

awful

If something is **awful**, it is very, very bad. This medicine tastes **awful**.

axe

An **axe** is a tool with a long handle and a sharp blade. People use **axes** to cut wood.

baby (babies)

A **baby** is a very young child.

back

1 Your **back** is the part of your body behind you, between your neck and your bottom.
2 Back is the opposite of front. Mum and dad sat in the front of the car and I sat in the **back**.

backwards

If you say the alphabet **backwards**, you start with Z and finish with A. I am walking **backwards** so I can't see where I'm going.

bad (worse, worst)

1 Bad means not good. Eating lots of chocolate is **bad** for you.
2 Food that is **bad** is too old to eat. This egg has gone **bad** – it smells terrible!

bag

You put things in a **bag** so you can carry them. **Bags** are made of plastic, paper, leather or cloth. We put the shopping in a **bag** to carry it home.

bake (baking, baked)

You **bake** food by cooking it in an oven. I am **baking** a cake for Jo's birthday.

balance (balancing, balanced)

When you **balance**, you keep steady without falling. Jenny is **balancing** on one leg.

ball

A **ball** is a round thing that you use in games. Throw the **ball** and I will try to catch it.

ballet *say *balay*

Ballet is a kind of dance.

balloon

A **balloon** is a kind of bag made of thin rubber or plastic. You fill a **balloon** with air or gas to make it float.

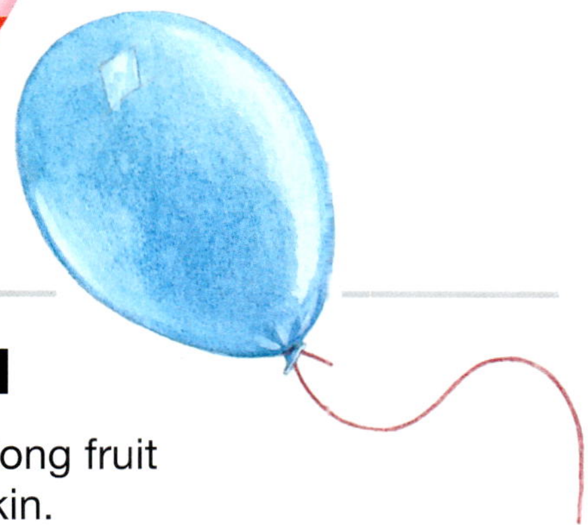

banana

A **banana** is a long fruit with a yellow skin.

band

1 A **band** is a group of people who play music together.
2 A **band** is also a thin piece of material around something. Put a rubber **band** around the letters to keep them together.

bandage

A **bandage** is a long piece of white cloth. You wrap a **bandage** around a cut on your body to keep it safe and clean.

bank

1 A **bank** is a place that looks after money for people.
2 A **bank** is also the land along the sides of a river.

bar

1 A **bar** is a long piece of metal.
2 A **bar** is also a piece of something hard like chocolate or soap.

bare

1 **Bare** means without any clothes on. Ned is walking around with **bare** feet.
2 **Bare** also means empty. Our house would look very **bare** without any furniture.

Another word that sounds like **bare** is **bear**.

bark

1 (barking, barked) When a dog **barks**, it makes a loud sound.
2 **Bark** is the rough outside of a tree trunk.

barn

A **barn** is a building on a farm, where the farmer keeps animals and things like hay. The horses sleep in the **barn**.

base

The **base** of something is the part at the bottom which it stands on. The lamp has a flat **base**.

baseball

Baseball is a game played by two teams with a bat and a ball.

basket

You can put things in a **basket** to carry them. **Baskets** are usually made of thin sticks or straw.

Jason is carrying a **basket** of fruit.

basketball

Basketball is a game played by two teams with a large ball. The players try to throw the ball into a high net.

bat

1 A **bat** is an animal like a mouse with wings. **Bats** fly at night.

2 A **bat** is also something that you use for hitting the ball in games like cricket and table tennis.

bath

A **bath** is a large container for water. You sit or lie in it to wash your whole body.

battery (batteries)

A **battery** is something that stores electricity. You put **batteries** in things like radios and watches to make them work.

beach (beaches)

A **beach** is a place next to the sea that is covered with sand or stones.

beak

A **beak** is the hard pointed part of a bird's mouth.

bear

A **bear** is a large wild animal with thick fur.

Another word that sounds like **bear** is **bare**.

beard

A **beard** is the hair that grows on a man's chin. My uncle has grown a **beard**.

beat (beating, beat, beaten)

If you **beat** somebody in a game or a race, you win.

beautiful

Something that is **beautiful** is lovely to look at, to hear or to smell. Those flowers are **beautiful**.

beaver

A **beaver** is a furry animal that lives in and by rivers. **Beavers** have strong, sharp front teeth and a flat tail for swimming.

bed

You lie on a **bed** when you sleep.

bee

A **bee** is a flying insect that makes honey.

beetle

A **beetle** is an insect with hard wings.

before

1 Before means at an earlier time. I have breakfast **before** I go to school.
2 Before also means in front of somebody or something. A comes **before** B in the alphabet.

begin (beginning, began, begun)

When something **begins**, it starts. What time does the film **begin**?

behave (behaving, behaved)

If you **behave** yourself, you are good and you do what somebody has told you to do.

behind

Behind means at the back of something. Billy is hiding **behind** the tree.

believe (believing, believed)

1 If you **believe** something, you are sure that it is true. Do you **believe** in ghosts?
2 If you **believe** somebody, you are sure that they are telling the truth.

bell

A **bell** makes a sound that rings when you hit it or press it.

Word play
Can you find the words that sound the same?

Answers at the back!

belong (belonging, belonged)

When something **belongs** to you, it is yours. Does this pen **belong** to you?

below

Below means under. Your mouth is **below** your nose.

belt

A **belt** is a long piece of cloth or leather that you can wear around your waist.

bend (bending, bent)

If you **bend** something, it is not straight any more. Amman is **bending** a piece of wire. Hugo is **bending** down to pick up his pencil.

berry (berries)

A **berry** is a small, soft fruit with seeds in it.

beside

Beside means next to. Bella is standing **beside** Billy.

best

The **best** person or thing is better than all the others. This is the **best** ice cream I have ever tasted!

better

1 Better is the way to say "more good" or "more well". Apples are **better** for you than sweets. I can draw **better** than my sister.
2 If you are feeling **better**, you are well again. I had a cold last week but I am feeling **better** now.

between

Between means in the middle.

Bella is standing **between** Aziz and Cara.

Tuesday comes **between** Monday and Wednesday.

bicycle

A **bicycle** has two wheels and pedals. A **bicycle** is often called a **bike**.

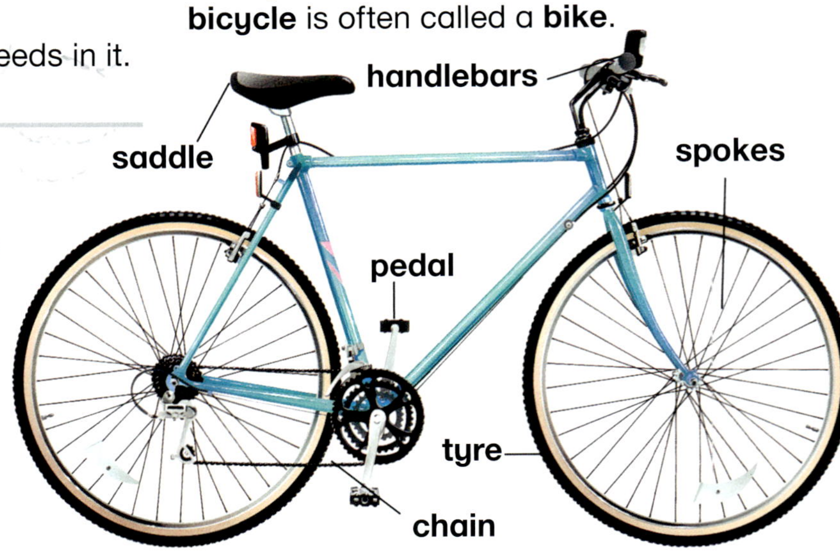

big (bigger, biggest)

Big means not small. This hat is too **big** for Saskia.

bike Look at **bicycle**.

bird

Birds have wings and feathers. Most **birds** can fly. (Look at the next page.)

birthday (birthdays)

Your **birthday** is a special day every year. You remember it because you were born on that date. My **birthday** is the first of May.

biscuit

A **biscuit** is a thin, flat, dry kind of cake.

bite (biting, bit, bitten)

When you **bite** something, you cut into it with your teeth.

Jenny is **biting** a carrot.

blade

A **blade** is the flat, sharp part of a knife.

blame (blaming, blamed)

If you **blame** somebody for something bad that happened, you think they made it happen. My brother **blamed** me for breaking his computer.

blanket

A **blanket** is a warm, thick cover for a bed.

blew Look at **blow**.

blind

1 Somebody who is **blind** cannot see at all.
2 A **blind** is something that you pull down to cover a window.

blink (blinking, blinked)

When you **blink**, you close your eyes and then open them again quickly.

block

1 A **block** is a thick piece of something like wood or stone, with straight sides.
2 (blocking, blocked) If something **blocks** a place, other people or things cannot get through.

A fallen tree was **blocking** the road.

Birds

▷ A **flamingo** has long legs, so its body stays dry when it walks on wet ground.

▷ An **eagle** has sharp claws called **talons** and a curved beak for tearing animals apart.

Feathers help to keep birds warm.

A bird has a hard **beak** or **bill** instead of teeth.

Birds have **claws** for holding onto things.

Birds build **nests** and lay their **eggs** there. The **chick** hatches out of the egg by cracking open the shell.

◁ **Ducks** paddle in the water with their **webbed feet**.

▷ **Parrots** have strong claws and short, curved beaks which they use for climbing about in trees.

◁ **Penguins** cannot fly, but they use their wings to help them swim.

blood

Blood is the red liquid that flows around inside your body.

blow (blowing, blew, blown)

1 When you **blow**, you push air out of your mouth. April is **blowing** out the candles on the birthday cake.
2 When the wind **blows**, the air moves.

boat

Boats carry people or things on water. A canoe is a kind of **boat**. Some **boats** have sails and some have engines. (Look at the next page.)

body (bodies)

Your **body** is the whole of you. People and animals have **bodies**. Your **body** can also be the whole of you apart from your head.

boil (boiling, boiled)

When water **boils**, it gets very hot. You can see bubbles in it, and steam coming off it.

bone

Your **bones** are the hard parts inside your body. All your **bones** together are called a skeleton.

book

A **book** is pieces of paper joined together inside a cover. Most **books** have words and pictures inside them. You are reading a **book** at the moment.

boot

1 A **boot** is a kind of shoe that covers your foot and part of your leg.
2 The **boot** of a car is the part where you can put things like boxes and bags.

bored

If you are **bored**, you feel tired and unhappy because you have nothing interesting to do.

born

When a baby is **born**, it starts to live outside its mother.

borrow (borrowing, borrowed)

If you **borrow** something from somebody, you take it for a short time and then you give it back. I often **borrow** books from the library.

both

Both means one and the other. Toby and Hugo are **both** wearing red shirts.

Boats

▽ A **raft** is a simple boat made from flat pieces of wood.

◁ **Sailing ships**, like this Chinese **junk**, are pushed along by the wind blowing against the sails.

▷ A **canoe** is moved through the water using **paddles**.

▽ A **cruise liner** is a kind of floating hotel.

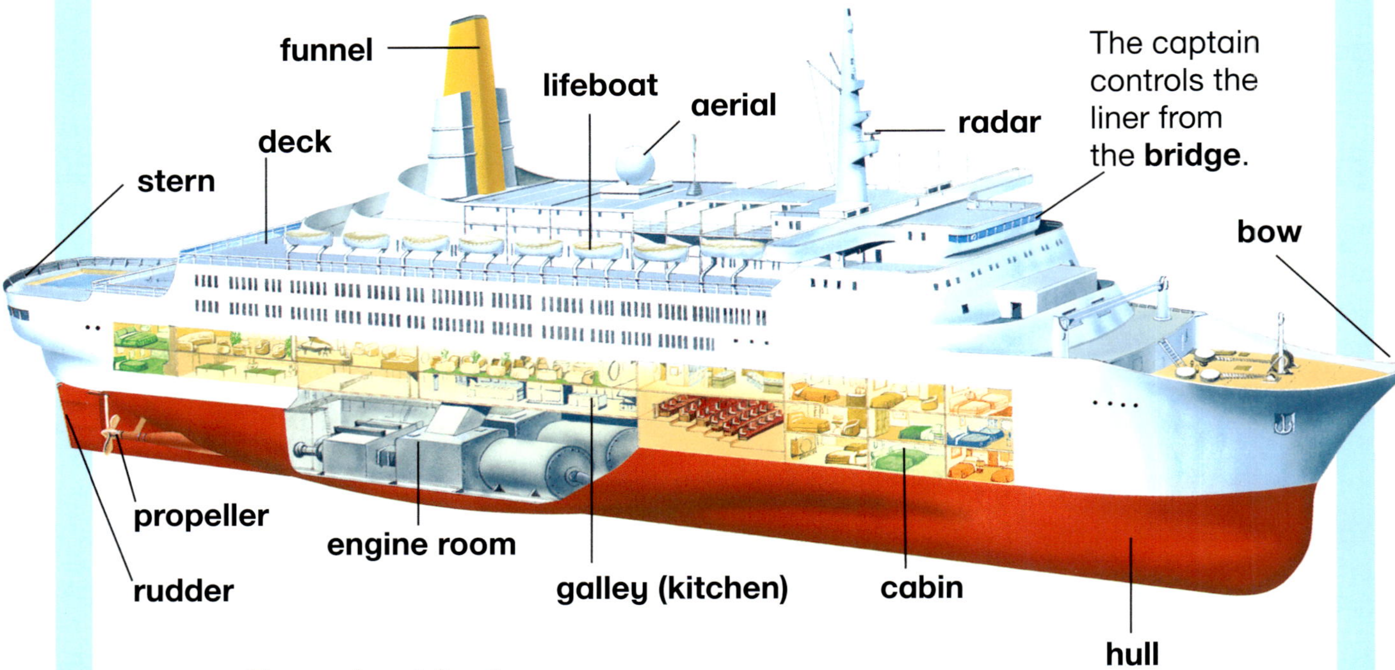

The captain controls the liner from the **bridge**.

How a boat floats
Drop a ball of modelling clay into a bowl of water, and watch it sink straight to the bottom. Try pressing the ball flat, and pulling up the sides to make a hull. Now your boat will float.

◁ **Paddle steamers** are driven by a big wheel at the back.

▷ **Tankers** are very large ships which carry liquids like oil, or gas.

bottle

Bottles are tall containers that hold liquids. They are made of glass or plastic.

bottom

1 The **bottom** of something is its lowest part. The ship sank to the **bottom** of the sea.
2 Your **bottom** is the part of your body that you sit on.

bought

Look at **buy**.

bounce (bouncing, bounced)

When a ball **bounces**, it springs up again after it hits the ground.

bow *rhymes with *so*

A **bow** is a kind of knot that you use to tie ribbon or string. Can you tie your laces in a **bow**?

bow *rhymes with *now*

(bowing, bowed)

If you **bow**, you bend your body and head forward and down. Actors **bow** at the end of a play.

bowl

A **bowl** is a deep, round dish for food or liquids. Barry poured soup into the **bowls**.

box (boxes)

You use a **box** for keeping things in. **Boxes** have straight sides and they are usually made of cardboard or wood. Naomi keeps all her toys in a toy **box**. You buy matches in a **matchbox**.

boy (boys)

A **boy** is a male child who will grow up to be a man.

brain

Your **brain** is inside your head. It controls the rest of your body and you use it for thinking and feeling.

branch (branches)

A **branch** is one of the parts of a tree that grow out from the trunk. Leaves grow from the **branches**.

brave

If you are **brave**, you show that you are not afraid, even though something hurts you or frightens you.

bread

Bread is food made from flour and baked in an oven. Can I have a slice of **bread** and butter, please?

breakfast

Breakfast is the first meal of the day.

breathe (breathing, breathed)

When we **breathe**, we take air into our bodies through our noses and mouths and then let it out again.

break (breaking, broke, broken)

If you **break** something, it goes into pieces or it stops working. I dropped my clock and **broke** it.

brick

A **brick** is a block of baked clay. We use **bricks** for building.

bridge

A **bridge** is something that is built over a river or a road so that people can get from one side to the other.

Word play
All these things begin with **b**.
What are they?

a part of a tree which grows out from the trunk

a special day every year that you remember because you were born on that day

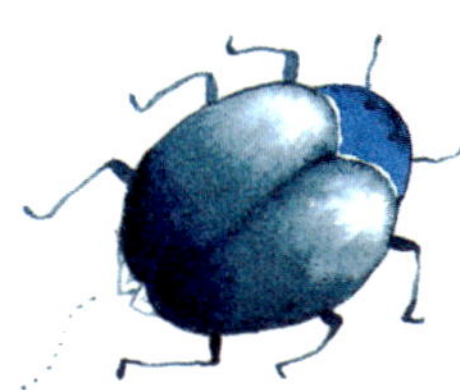

a flower or leaf that is not open yet

an insect with hard wings

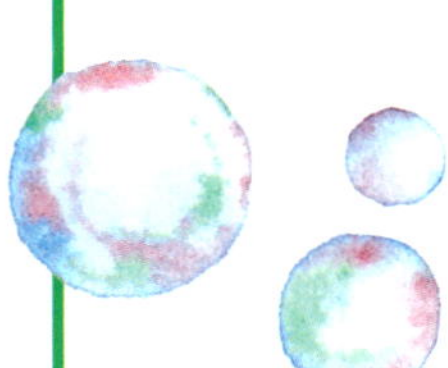

a small, light ball of soap or liquid with air inside

Now take the third letter of each of the words you found and mix them up to spell something beginning with **b** that you can see on some men's faces!

Answers on page 176.

bright

1 Bright lights shine very strongly. The sun is very **bright** today because there are no clouds in the sky.
2 Bright colours are very clear and easy to see. My bike is **bright** red.
3 A person who is **bright** is clever.

bring (bringing, brought)

If you **bring** something, you carry it with you when you come. I **bring** sandwiches with me to school every day.

broke Look at **break**.

broken Look at **break**.

brother

Your **brother** is a boy who has the same mother and father as you.

brought Look at **bring**.

brush (brushes)

A **brush** is a tool that has a lot of hairs joined to a handle. You use different kinds of **brushes** for doing different jobs. You make your hair tidy with a **hairbrush** and you paint with a **paintbrush**.

bubble

A **bubble** is a small, light ball of soap or liquid with air inside.

Hugo is blowing **bubbles**.

bucket

You use a **bucket** for carrying liquids. **Buckets** have handles and they are made of plastic or metal.

bud

A **bud** is a flower or a leaf that is not completely open.

build (building, built)

If you **build** something, you make it by putting parts together. The **builders** are **building** a wall with bricks.

building

Houses, schools and hospitals are all **buildings**. A **building** has walls and a roof.

built Look at **build**.

bulb

1 A **bulb** is the glass part of a lamp.
2 A **bulb** is also the round root of a plant that grows under the ground. Tulips grow from **bulbs**.

bull

Cows and **bulls** are cattle. The **bull** is the male.

bulldozer

A **bulldozer** is a big, heavy machine that pushes dirt and rocks and makes land flat.

bunch (bunches)

A **bunch** is a group of things that are joined or tied together. I gave Bella a **bunch** of flowers on her birthday. We ate a whole **bunch** of grapes.

burn (burning, burnt or burned)

1 If something is **burning**, it is on fire.
2 If you **burn** something, you hurt or damage it with fire or heat. Don't touch the iron or you will **burn** your hand.

burst (bursting, burst)

If something **bursts**, it breaks open suddenly.

If you stick a pin in a balloon, it will **burst**.

bus (buses)

A **bus** is a big machine that can carry a lot of people from place to place. It has four wheels and an engine.

bush (bushes)

A **bush** is a small tree with a lot of branches that grows close to the ground.

busy (busier, busiest)

1 If you are **busy**, you have a lot of things to do. I can't help you now because I am too **busy**.
2 If a place is **busy**, a lot of things are happening there.

We live on a very **busy** street.

butter

Butter is soft, yellow food that is made from cream and milk from a cow. You can spread it on bread or use it in cooking.

butterfly (butterflies)

A **butterfly** is an insect with four pretty wings. **Butterflies** grow from caterpillars.

button

A **button** is a small, round thing on clothes. You push it through a hole called a **buttonhole** to keep your clothes done up.

buy (buying, bought)

When you **buy** something, you pay money so you can have it. I have **bought** a present for my friend because it is her birthday tomorrow.

cabbage

A **cabbage** is a vegetable with big, green leaves.

cage

A **cage** is a box or a room with bars. Animals and birds are often kept in **cages**. My hamster lives in a **cage**.

cake

A **cake** is a food made with flour, eggs, butter and sugar and baked in an oven. My friend baked a **cake** for my birthday.

calendar

A **calendar** is a list of all the days, weeks and months of a year. You will find today's date on a **calendar**.

calf (calves)

A **calf** is a young cow or bull.

call (calling, called)

1 If you **call** somebody, you speak loudly so that they will come to you, or you telephone them.
2 When somebody is **called** something, they have that name. My dog is **called** Poppy.

calves Look at **calf**.

camel

A **camel** is a big animal that can carry people or things in hot, dry countries. Some **camels** have one hump on their backs, and some have two.

camera

You take photographs with a **camera**.

camp

A **camp** is a place where people live in tents or huts for a short time.

can

A **can** is a metal container. You sometimes buy food like soup and vegetables in **cans**. Some drinks also come in **cans**.

candle

A **candle** is a stick of wax with a piece of string, called a wick, through the middle. The wick burns to give light.

canoe

A **canoe** is a small, narrow boat. You use a paddle to move it along.

cap

1 A **cap** is a small hat with a pointed part, called a peak, at the front.
2 A **cap** is also a small lid. Somebody forgot to put the **cap** back on the toothpaste.

car

A **car** is a machine that you ride in. It has four wheels and an engine to make it go.

card

A **card** is a piece of thick paper. On special days like birthdays, people send **cards** with pictures and words on them. You can use other **cards** to play games.

cardboard

Cardboard is thick paper that does not bend easily. It is used to make boxes.

care (caring, cared)

If you **care** for somebody or something, you look after them well. People who do not **care** for their pets properly are cruel.

careful

If you are **careful**, you think about what you are doing so that you do it safely and well. Be **careful**! Don't drop those glasses!

carpet

A **carpet** is a large, thick cloth that covers the floor.

carrot

A **carrot** is a long, orange-coloured vegetable that grows under the ground.

carry (carries, carrying, carried)

When you **carry** something, you pick it up and take it to another place.

Isis is **carrying** some books.

Cars

△ A **four-wheel drive** is good for driving on rough ground.

▷ **Taxis** carry people around towns for money.

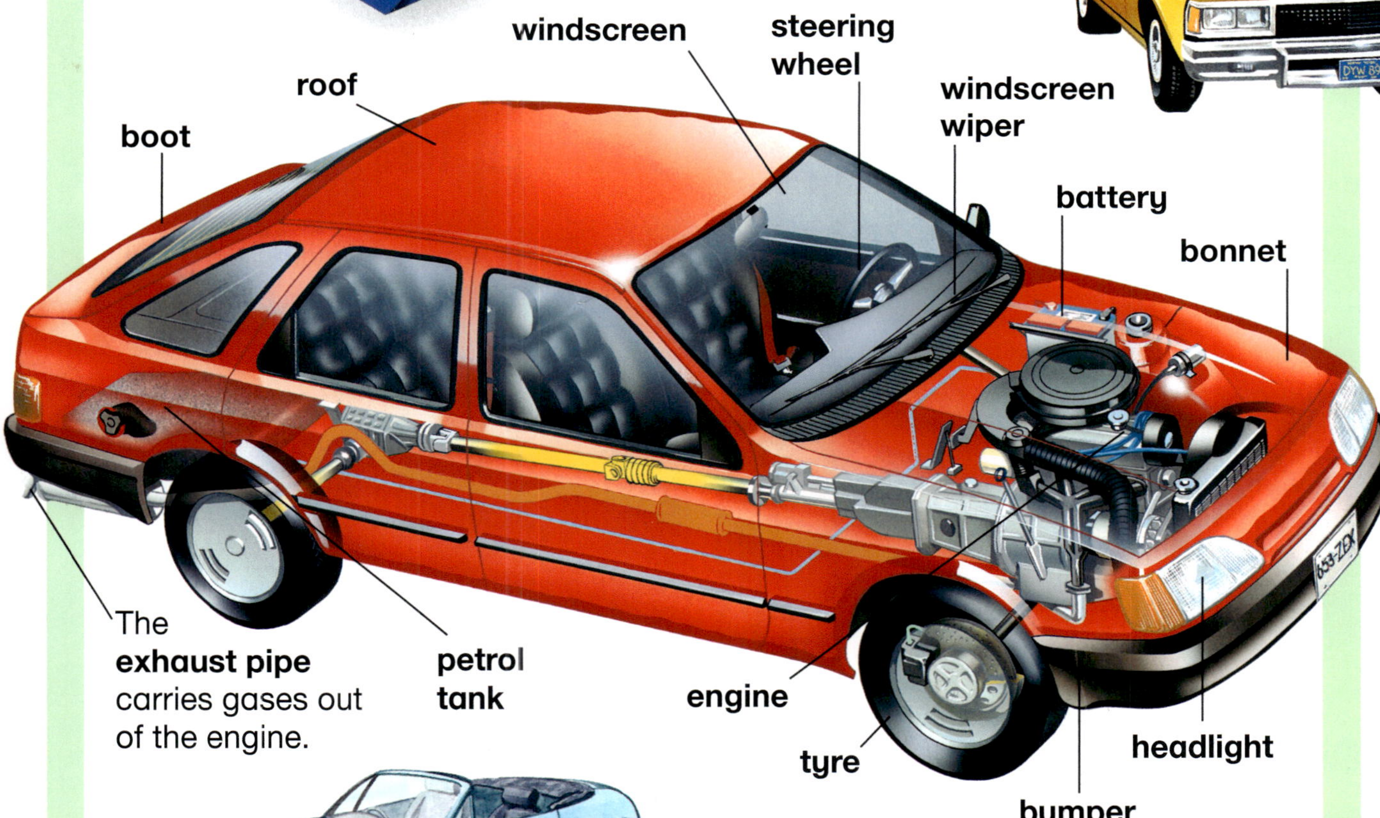

△ A **convertible** has a soft roof that can be folded down.

◁ A **pick-up** is a small truck with low sides.

▽ **Limousines** are large and very comfortable inside.

▷ An **estate** car has plenty of room in the back for carrying things.

carton

A **carton** is a cardboard or plastic box. Food and drink are packed in **cartons**.

cartoon

A **cartoon** is a short, funny film using drawings, or a funny drawing in a newspaper.

cassette

A **cassette** is a plastic box with a tape inside it which stores sound and sometimes pictures.

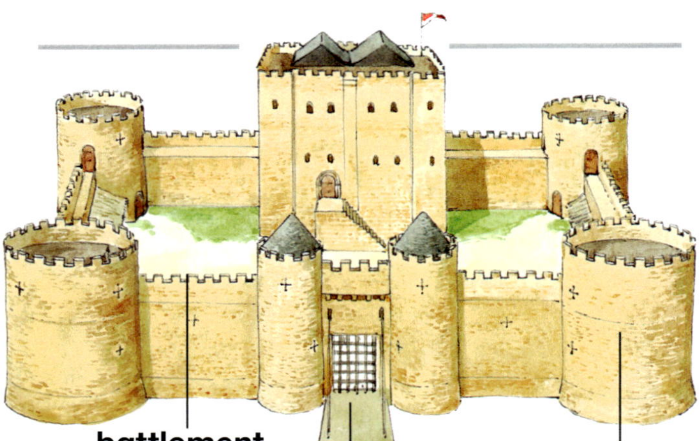

castle

Castles were built long ago. They had thick high walls to keep the people inside safe from other people who wanted to attack them.

cat

A **cat** is a furry animal with sharp claws. People keep small **cats** as pets. A young **cat** is called a kitten. Large **cats** like lions and tigers live in the wild.

catch (catches, catching, caught)

1 When you **catch** somebody or something that is moving, you take hold of it. If I throw the ball, will you **catch** it?
2 When you **catch** an illness, you get it. Cathy has **caught** a cold.

caterpillar

Caterpillars look like furry worms with legs. They change into butterflies and moths.

cattle

Cattle are large animals that are kept on farms for their milk and meat. Cows and bulls are **cattle**.

caught

Look at **catch**.

cauliflower

A **cauliflower** is a vegetable with a white middle and green leaves on the outside.

cave

A **cave** is a big hole in the side of a mountain or under the ground. People once lived in **caves**.

ceiling

The **ceiling** is the top part of a room. The lamp is hanging from the **ceiling**.

centre

The **centre** of something is the middle part. In the game, we all made a circle and Lucy stood in the **centre**.

century (centuries)

A **century** is a hundred years. We are living at the end of the twentieth **century**.

cereal

A **cereal** is a kind of food that we eat for breakfast. **Cereals** are made from the seeds of different plants, like rice and wheat.

chain

A **chain** is made of metal rings joined together.

chair

A **chair** is a seat with a back, for one person to sit on.

change (changing, changed)

1 When something **changes**, it becomes different. Water **changes** into ice when it gets very cold.
2 When you **change**, you put on different clothes. Isis has to **change** before she can go to the party.

chase (chasing, chased)

If you **chase** something or somebody, you go after them and try to catch them.

cheap

Something that is **cheap** does not cost a lot of money. This toy car is very **cheap**.

check (checking, checked)

When you **check** something, you look at it again to make sure that it is right. Please **check** my spelling.

cheek

Your **cheeks** are the soft parts on each side of your face.

cheerful

If you are **cheerful**, you feel happy.

cheese

Cheese is white or yellow food made from milk.

chest

1 A **chest** is a large strong box with a lid.
2 Your **chest** is the front part of your body between your neck and your stomach.

chew (chewing, chewed)

When you **chew** food, you use your teeth to make it soft. The dog **chewed** my shoe.

Word play
The word for more than one **child** is **children**. In this dictionary, you can see it written in brackets ( ) after the word **child**.

Do you know the word for more than one:

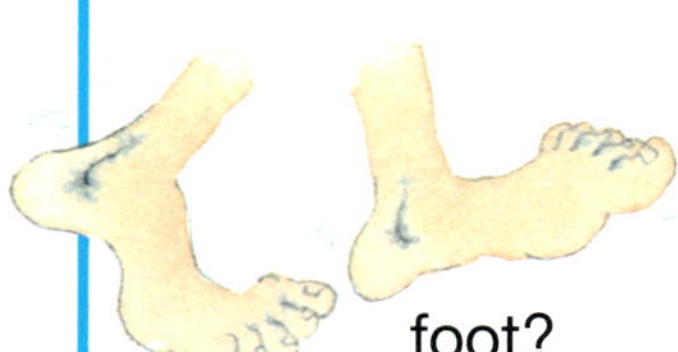

foot?

woman?

mouse?

calf?

city?

Use the dictionary to check your answers!

Answers at the back!

chick

A **chick** is a baby bird.

chicken

A **chicken** is a bird which lays the eggs we eat.

chief

A **chief** is the leader of a group of people. A **chief** tells other people what to do.

child (children)

A **child** is a boy or a girl. **Children** grow up to be men and women.

chimney (chimneys)

A **chimney** is a large pipe above a fire that lets smoke and gas go outside into the air.

chin

Your **chin** is the part of your face that is under your mouth.

chocolate

Chocolate is a sweet, brown food. It is used for making sweets and cakes.

choose (choosing, chose, chosen)

When you **choose** something, you take it because it is the one you want. Richard is **choosing** a new shirt.

circle

A **circle** is a round shape like a ring.

circus (circuses)

A **circus** is a group of people like acrobats and clowns who travel around giving shows in different places.

city (cities)

A **city** is a very big town. London is a **city**.

clap (clapping, clapped)

When you **clap**, you hit your hands together to make a loud noise. We all **clapped** at the end of the play.

class (classes)

A **class** is a group of pupils who are learning together at school. There are thirty children in my **class**.

claw

A **claw** is a sharp, curved nail on an animal's foot.

clay

Clay is a special kind of earth that becomes hard when it is dry. **Clay** is used for making things like bricks and pots.

clean

1 Something that is **clean** does not have any dirt or marks on it. My hands are **clean** – I have just washed them.
2 (cleaning, cleaned)
When you **clean** something, you take the dirt or marks away. I am **cleaning** my bike.

clear

1 You can see through something that is **clear**. Most glass is **clear**.
2 If something is **clear**, it is easy to see, to understand or to hear. The photo will not be very **clear** if you move the camera when you are taking it.

Clothes

tights
sleeve
shorts
shirt
T-shirt
dress
vest
collar
jumper/
sweater
button
blouse
pocket
belt
pants
shoelace
jeans
cuff
skirt
shoe
sock
pyjamas
dressing
gown
hat
swimsuit
cap
scarf
coat
leotard
gloves
tracksuit
slipper
swimming
trunks
trousers
boot
trainer

clever

Somebody who is **clever** can learn and understand things quickly and well. It was **clever** of you to do the puzzle so quickly.

cliff

A **cliff** is a high hill with one side that goes straight down. Many **cliffs** are by the sea.

climb (climbing, climbed)

If you **climb** something, you move up using your hands and feet to hold on.

Jason is **climbing** the ladder.

clock

A **clock** is a machine that tells you what time it is.

close (closing, closed)

*say *kloze*

When you **close** something, you shut it. Please **close** the door after you.

close *say *klose*

Something that is **close** is near. I live **close** to my school.

closed

If something is **closed**, it is not open. The shop is **closed** on Sundays.

cloth

Clothes are made of **cloth**. A lot of **cloth** is made of wool or cotton.

clothes

Your **clothes** are all the things you wear. Skirts, trousers and socks are **clothes**.

cloud

A **cloud** is millions of tiny drops of water that make a grey or white shape floating in the sky. The water from **clouds** sometimes falls as rain.

clown

A **clown** is a person who does funny things to make people laugh. **Clowns** paint their faces and dress up in strange clothes.

clue

A **clue** is something that helps to find the answer to a problem or mystery.

The detective is looking for **clues** that will help him find the thief.

coast

The **coast** is where the land meets the sea.

coat

You wear a **coat** on top of your other clothes to keep you warm on cold days.

cocoon

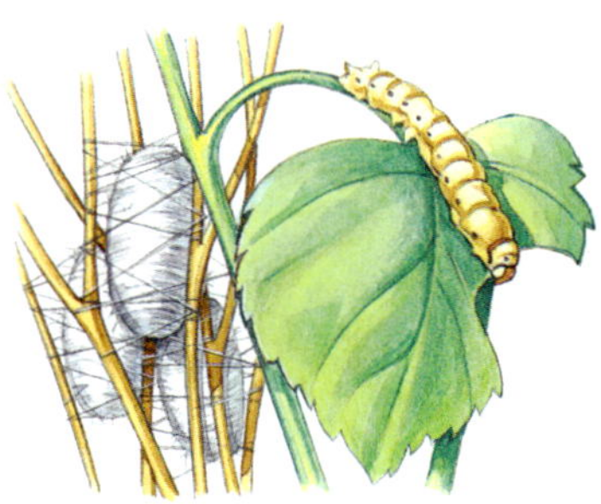

A **cocoon** is a small ball of threads made by a caterpillar. The caterpillar lives in the **cocoon** before it changes into a moth.

coffee

Coffee is a hot drink that is made by adding water to a brown powder. This powder is made from part of the **coffee** tree.

coin

A **coin** is a piece of money made of metal.

cold

1 Cold means not hot. Ice and snow are **cold**. If you feel **cold**, put a jumper on.

2 When you have a **cold**, you feel ill and you sneeze and cough.

collar

The **collar** of something like a shirt or a coat is the part that goes around your neck.

collect (collecting, collected)

When you **collect** things, you save up a lot of things because you are interested in them. Charlie is **collecting** shells.

colour

Red, yellow, blue and green are **colours**.

comfortable

Something that is **comfortable** is nice to be in or to wear. I slept well because the bed is very **comfortable**.

comic

A **comic** is a kind of magazine that tells stories in pictures.

Colours

Red, yellow and blue are the **primary colours**. We mix these colours to make other colours.

red yellow blue

Red and yellow make **orange**.

Yellow and blue make **green**.

Red and blue make **purple**.

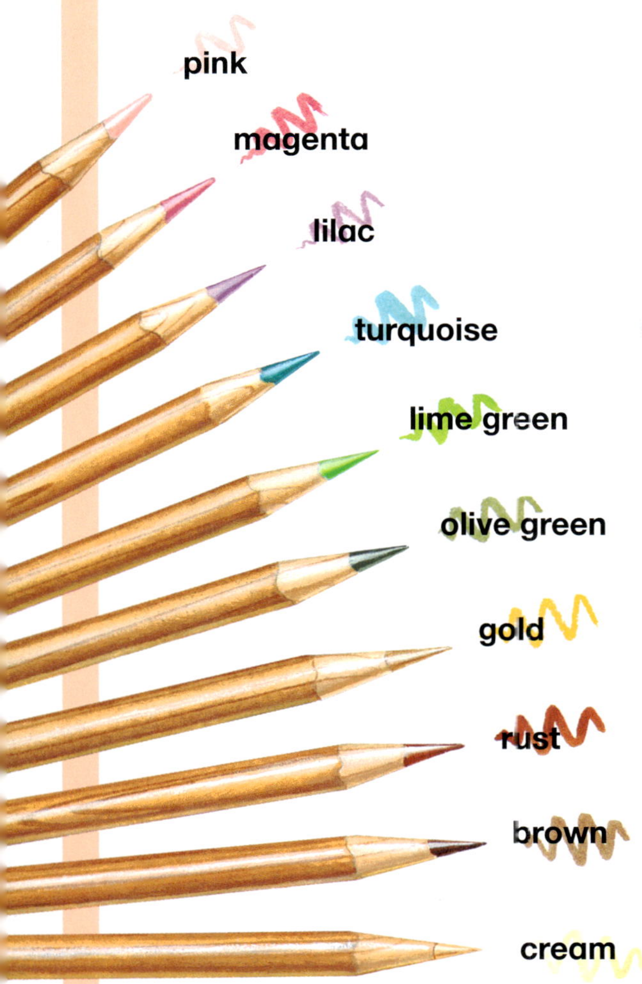

compact disc

A **compact disc** is a flat, round piece of silver-coloured plastic that has music or words stored on it. We also call it a **CD**.

complete

If something is **complete**, it has no parts missing. We saw a **complete** skeleton of a dinosaur in the museum.

computer

A **computer** is a machine that can solve problems quickly, store information, and control other machines.

confuse (confusing, confused)

To **confuse** means to mix up somebody's ideas, so that they cannot understand. My sister explained how to play the game but she went too quickly and I got **confused**.

container

A **container** is something for putting things in. Jars, bottles and boxes are **containers**.

contest

A **contest** is way of finding out who is the best at doing something. My brother won the swimming **contest** at school.

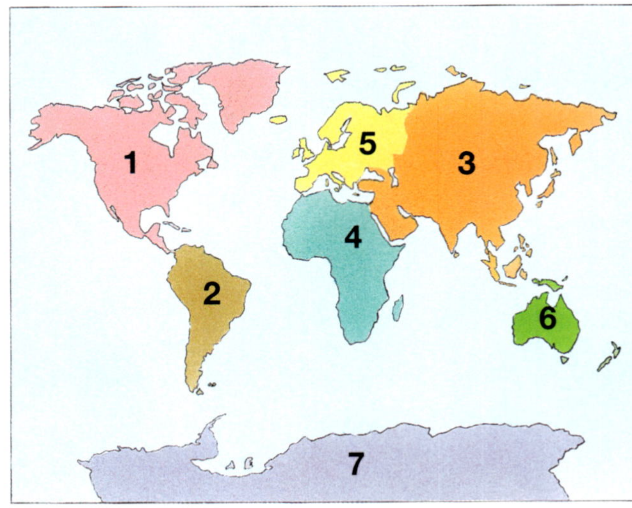

continent

The **continents** are the seven main areas of land of the world. They are **1** North America, **2** South America, **3** Asia, **4** Africa, **5** Europe, **6** Australia and **7** Antarctica.

continue (continuing, continued)

When you **continue** doing something, you keep on doing it. Matt **continued** watching television after his dad told him to go to bed.

control (controlling, controlled)

If you **control** something, you make it do what you want. She can't **control** her dog.

cook (cooking, cooked)

When you **cook** food, you heat it to make it ready to eat. You **cook** food on top of a **cooker** or inside it.

cool

If something is **cool**, it is quite cold. It was warm yesterday, but it is **cooler** today.

copy (copying, copied)

When you **copy** something, you make it look or sound just like something else. Isis's mum drew a picture of a horse and Isis **copied** it.

corn

Corn is plants like wheat that farmers grow for their seeds, called grain. **Corn** can be made into flour.

corner

A **corner** is a place where two roads, edges or walls meet.

corridor

A **corridor** is a long, narrow place inside a building that has doors on each side.

cost (costing, cost)

The amount you pay for something is how much it **costs**. How much did your new game **cost**?

costume

A **costume** is all the clothes that an actor wears. Katie is wearing a tiger **costume** for the school play.

cotton

1 Cotton is light cloth that is made from the soft white stuff that grows on a **cotton** plant.
2 Cotton is also thread that people use for sewing.

cough *say *koff* (coughing, coughed)

When you **cough**, you make a sudden, loud noise in your throat.

Word play
Change the order of the letters to spell the names of six animals in this dictionary that begin with **c**.

tac reoccolid kichenc falc malec piterlarcal

Answers on page 176.

count (counting, counted)

When you **count**, you say numbers one after another in the right order. **Count** from one to a hundred. You also **count** when you add up a number of things. Can you **count** how many stars there are in the sky?

country (countries)

1 A **country** is a part of the world with its own people and laws. Japan and Spain are **countries**.

2 The **country** is the land outside towns where there are fields, woods and farms. We live in the **country**.

cousin

Your **cousin** is the child of your uncle or aunt.

cover
(covering, covered)

When you **cover** something, you put something else over it to hide it or to keep it safe or warm.

Alice is **covering** her teddy.

cow

A **cow** is a large animal that gives us milk. A young **cow** is called a calf.

crack

A **crack** is a thin line on something where it is nearly broken. There is a **crack** in this plate.

crane

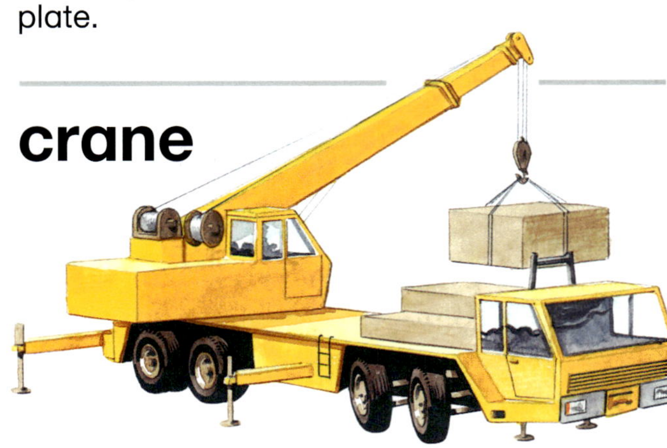

A **crane** is a tall machine that lifts and moves heavy things.

crash (crashes, crashing, crashed)

When something **crashes**, it hits something else with a very loud noise.

crawl (crawling, crawled)

When you **crawl**, you move along on your hands and knees.

crayon

A **crayon** is a kind of soft pencil for drawing and colouring. **Crayons** are often made of wax.

cream

Cream is the thick part on the top of milk. Would you like **cream** with your cake?

creature

A **creature** is any animal. A dragon is a strange **creature** that you can read about in stories.

creep (creeping, crept)

When you **creep**, you move quietly and slowly, trying not to be seen. The cat is **creeping** towards the bird.

cricket

1 Cricket is a game for two teams of eleven players. **Cricket** is played with a bat and ball.
2 A **cricket** is a jumping insect like a grasshopper that makes a loud sound.

cried Look at **cry**.

cries Look at **cry**.

crocodile

A **crocodile** is a large animal with a long body and big, sharp teeth. It lives in rivers in some hot countries. **Crocodiles** are reptiles.

crooked

Something that is **crooked** is not straight. The old man's back was **crooked** so he had to walk with a stick.

crop

Crops are plants that farmers grow as food.

cross

1 If you are **cross**, you feel angry about something.
2 (crosses, crossing, crossed) To **cross** means to go from one side to the other. Look both ways before you **cross** the road.
3 (crosses) A **cross** is a mark like + or X.

crowd

A **crowd** is a lot of people in one place. I was looking for my friend in the **crowd**.

crown

A **crown** is a ring of gold and jewels that kings and queens wear on their heads.

cruel (crueller, cruellest)

Somebody who is **cruel** hurts other people or animals. The witch in the story was very **cruel** to her cat.

crumb

A **crumb** is a tiny bit of cake or bread.

cry (cries, crying, cried)

When you **cry**, you have tears falling from your eyes.

cub

A **cub** is a young bear, lion, tiger, fox or wolf.

cube

A **cube** is a shape with six square sides. Dice are shaped like **cubes**.

cup

A **cup** is a small container with a handle. You drink things like tea and coffee from **cups**.

curl

A **curl** is a piece of hair in a curved shape. Amman has **curly** hair.

curtain

Curtains are pieces of cloth that you pull across a window to cover it.

curve (curving, curved)

When a line turns or bends one way, it **curves**.

The letter C is a **curved** shape.

cushion

A **cushion** is a bag filled with something soft. You put a **cushion** on a seat to make it more comfortable to sit on.

cut (cutting, cut)

You use scissors or a knife to **cut** things into pieces. Jenny is **cutting** out a picture from her comic.

daisy (daisies)

A **daisy** is a flower with white petals and a yellow middle.

damage (damaging, damaged)

If you **damage** something, you spoil or break it. The building was badly **damaged** by the fire.

damp

If something is **damp**, it is a little wet. Your shirt isn't dry yet. It's still **damp**.

dance
(dancing, danced)

When you **dance**, you move your body in time to music.

danger

When there is **danger**, something bad may happen.

The notice said "**Danger**! Keep out."

dangerous

Something that is **dangerous** can hurt you. It is **dangerous** to ride a bike at night without any lights.

dark

1 Dark means without any light. It is **dark** at night.
2 Dark hair is brown or black.

date

The **date** is the day, the month and sometimes the year when something happens. Today's **date** is the thirteenth of June.

daughter

Somebody's **daughter** is a girl or a woman who is their child.

day (days)

1 A **day** is a time of 24 hours. Every **day** starts at midnight and ends the next midnight. There are seven **days** in a week.
2 Day is also the time when it is light outside.

dead

A person, an animal or a plant that is **dead** is not living any more.

This plant is **dead** because you forgot to water it.

deaf

A person who is **deaf** cannot hear very well or cannot hear at all.

dear

1 You put **dear** before a person's name when you are writing a letter.
2 Something that is **dear** costs a lot of money. I'm not buying that because I think it's too **dear**.

Another word that sounds like **dear** is **deer**.

decide (deciding, decided)

When you **decide**, you make up your mind about something. I can't **decide** which book to buy.

deep

Something that is **deep** goes down a long way from the top. When I can swim better I will be able to go in the **deep** end of the pool with my sister.

deer (deer)

Another word that sounds like **deer** is **dear**.

A **deer** is an animal that can run fast. **Deer** have long legs and the males have big horns called antlers on their heads.

delicious

Something that is **delicious** is very good to eat. This cake is **delicious**.

deliver (delivering, delivered)

If somebody **delivers** something, they bring it to you. The postwoman **delivers** letters to our house every day.

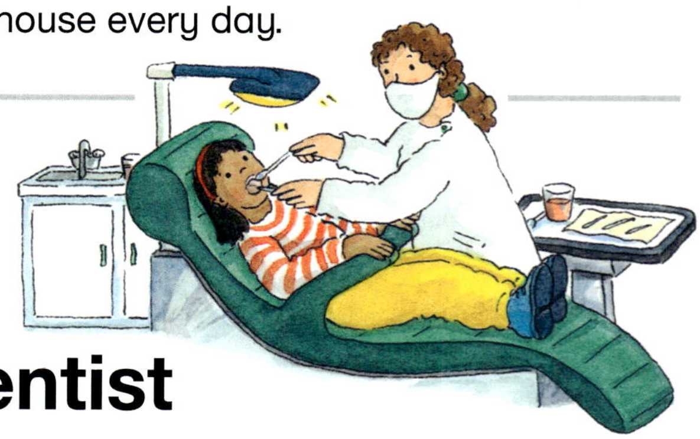

dentist

A **dentist** is a doctor who looks after people's teeth.

describe (describing, described)

When you **describe** somebody or something, you say what it is like. Can you **describe** the place where you live?

desert

A **desert** is very dry land where not many plants can grow.

design (designing, designed)

To **design** means to prepare a plan of something to show how it will be made. At school we are **designing** all sorts of costumes for our play.

desk

A **desk** is a kind of table with drawers. You can sit at a **desk** to read and write.

detective

A **detective** is a person who tries to find out who did something such as a robbery. The **detective** is looking for clues.

diamond

A **diamond** is a very hard jewel that looks like clear glass. My mum's ring has a big **diamond** in it.

diary (diaries)

A **diary** is a book where you write what happens every day. I make notes about important things in my **diary** so that I don't forget about them.

dice

Dice are small blocks made of wood or plastic with a different number of spots on each side. You use **dice** for playing games.

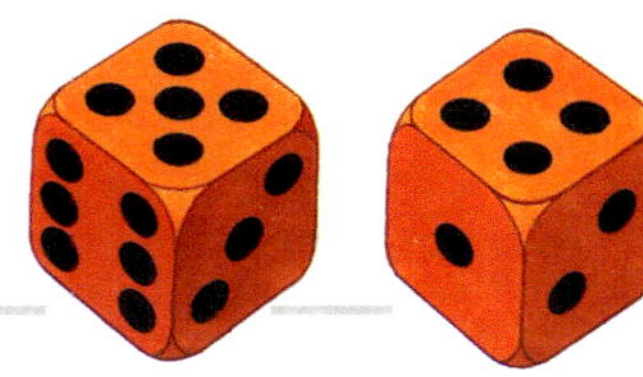

dictionary (dictionaries)

A **dictionary** is a book where you can find what words mean and how to spell them. You are reading a **dictionary** now.

die (dying, died)

When a person, an animal or a plant **dies**, it stops living. We would all **die** without water.

different

Different means not the same. David and Tom's shirts are **different** colours. One is blue, and the other one is red.

difficult

Something that is **difficult** is not easy to do. That high wall would be very **difficult** to climb over.

Dinosaurs

◁The sharp points on the end of **Stegosaurus**'s tail helped to protect it from attackers.

◁**Iguanodon** was a big and gentle plant-eater.

▷ **Triceratops** used its big horns to frighten off meat-eaters.

▽ **Apatosaurus** had a long neck so it could reach leaves at the tops of trees.

▽ Fierce **Velociraptor** had sharp claws and teeth and moved very fast.

▷ **Tyrannosaurus rex** had a huge mouth with very sharp teeth.

dig (digging, dug)

If you **dig**, you make a hole in the ground by moving soil or sand. You usually use a spade for **digging**.

dinner

Dinner is the main meal of the day. Some people eat their **dinner** in the evening and other people eat it in the middle of the day.

dinosaur

A **dinosaur** is an animal that lived millions of years ago. There were many different kinds of **dinosaur**.

Dinosaur comes from two Greek words that mean 'terrible lizard'.

dip (dipping, dipped)

To **dip** means to put something in liquid, then quickly take it out again. Flora **dipped** her finger in the cream and then tasted it.

direction

A **direction** is the way that a person or thing is going. We got lost because we went in the wrong **direction**.

dirt

Dirt is mud, soil or marks that must be cleaned off. Our boots were covered in **dirt** after our walk in the fields, so we took them off before we went into the house.

dirty (dirtier, dirtiest)

Something that is **dirty** is covered with dirt or marks. My white trousers got **dirty** when I sat down on the ground. Please go and wash your **dirty** hands.

disappear (disappearing, disappeared)

When something **disappears**, it suddenly goes away. The magician made the rabbit **disappear**.

disappointed

If you are **disappointed**, you are unhappy because something you were hoping for did not happen. I was **disappointed** when we couldn't go to the fair.

discover (discovering, discovered)

When you **discover** something, you find out about it or you see it for the first time. We **discovered** a secret hiding place in the hollow trunk of a tree.

disguise

A **disguise** is something that you do to change the way you look, so that other people will not know who you are.

dish (dishes)

You use a **dish** for cooking food or putting it on the table. We put the fruit salad in a big **dish.**

distance

The **distance** between two places is how far they are from each other. The **distance** between the swimming-pool and my school is three kilometres.

disturb (disturbing, disturbed)

If somebody **disturbs** you, they stop you doing what you are doing at the moment.

Please don't **disturb** Jesse because he's trying to read.

dive (diving, dived)

If you **dive** into water, you jump in with your hands and head first.

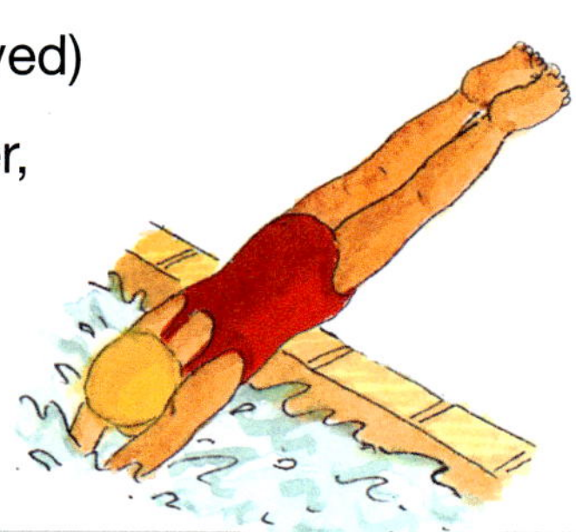

divide (dividing, divided)

1 When you **divide** something, you make it go into smaller parts. Our teacher **divided** us into two teams for the game.
2 When you **divide** numbers, you see how many times one number will go into another. Eight **divided** by four is two.

doctor

A **doctor** is a person who helps you to get better when you are ill.

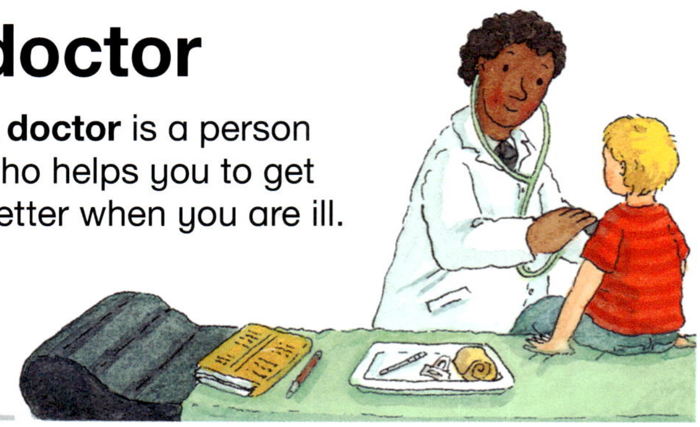

dog

A **dog** is an animal that people keep as a pet. **Dogs** are also used to do work, like guarding buildings and hunting. A young **dog** is called a puppy.

doll

A **doll** is a toy that looks like a small person.

dolphin

A **dolphin** is an animal that lives in the sea. **Dolphins** look like fish but they are really mammals.

drag (dragging, dragged)

If you **drag** something, you pull it along slowly. Katey is **dragging** her school bag along behind her.

donkey (donkeys)

A **donkey** is an animal that looks like a small horse with long ears.

dragon

A **dragon** is an animal that you can read about in stories. **Dragons** have wings and long tails. Their bodies are covered in scales and they breathe fire.

drank Look at **drink**.

door

You open a **door** when you go in and out of a room or a building.

dot

A **dot** is a small, round spot, like this: 

down

Down means from a higher to a lower place. We ran **down** the hill.

Word play
Trace this puzzle, then join the dots by following the letters in the order that they come in the alphabet to see a picture of something beginning with **d**.

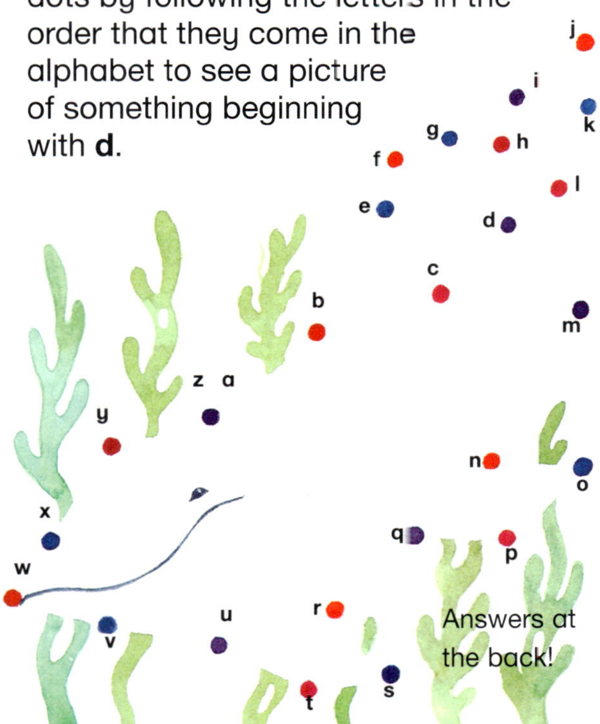

Answers at the back!

draw
(drawing, drew, drawn)

If you **draw**, you make a picture with a pencil, pen or crayon. Thomas is **drawing** a picture of his family.

drawer

A **drawer** is a box that you can push into and pull out of a piece of furniture. I keep my socks in the top **drawer** of the chest of **drawers**.

drawing

A **drawing** is a picture that you make with a pencil, pen or crayon.

Word play
How many little words can you find inside this word, keeping the letters in the same order?

drawing

Answers at the back!

drawn
Look at **draw**.

dream
(dreaming, dreamt or dreamed)

When you **dream**, pictures and thoughts go through your mind. You **dream** when you are asleep. Last night I **dreamt** that I was flying like a bird.

dress

1 (dresses) A **dress** is a skirt and top joined together. Girls and women wear **dresses**.
2 (dressing, dressed) When you get **dressed**, you put your clothes on. In the mornings, I get up, have a wash and then get **dressed**.

drew
Look at **draw**.

drill

A **drill** is a tool that you use for making holes. The man is using an electric **drill** to make a hole in the wall.

drink
(drinking, drank, drunk)

When you **drink**, you take liquid into your body through your mouth.

Emma is **drinking** a glass of water.

drip (dripping, dripped)

When a liquid **drips**, it falls in small drops.
Water is **dripping** through a hole in the roof.

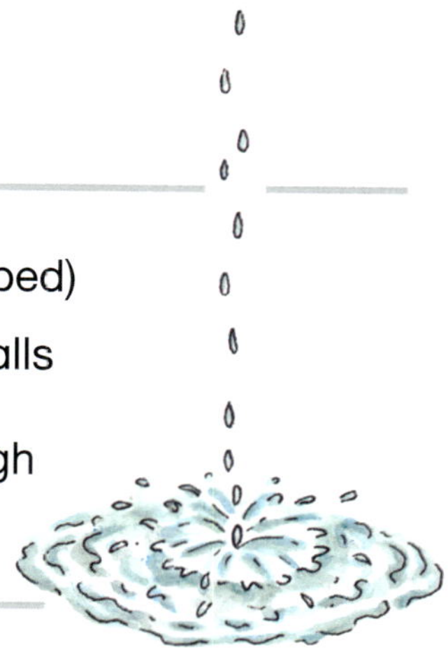

drive (driving, drove, driven)

To **drive** means to make something like a car or a bus move along. My mum **drives** a bus. She's a bus **driver**.

drop

1 (dropping, dropped)
If you **drop** something, you let it fall by accident. She **dropped** a plate and it smashed.
2 A **drop** of a liquid is a very small amount. Rain is made of small **drops** of water.

drove Look at **drive**.

drown (drowning, drowned)

If somebody **drowns**, they die because they are under water and they cannot breathe.

drum

A **drum** is a musical instrument that you hit with sticks or with your hands to make a sound.

drunk Look at **drink**.

dry

1 (drier, driest) Something that is **dry** is not wet. You can't put your shirt on because it's not **dry** yet.
2 (dries, drying, dried) When you **dry** something, you make it dry. You **dry** yourself with a towel after a bath or shower.

duck

A **duck** is a bird that can swim as well as fly. We fed the **ducks** on the pond.

dug Look at **dig**.

dull

Dull means not bright. It is a **dull**, cloudy day, but yesterday it was sunny.

dust

Dust is small bits of dry dirt like powder.

duvet *say *doovay*

A **duvet** is a thick cover that keeps you warm in bed. Many **duvets** have feathers inside them.

dying Look at **die**.

early (earlier, earliest)

1 Early means near the beginning of something. The birds start singing **early** in the morning.
2 Early also means before the usual time. We arrived at the show **early** so we could get the best seats.

earn (earning, earned)

To **earn** means to get money for work that you do. Karen sometimes **earns** money by taking her neighbour's dog for walks.

each

Each means every thing or every person. The teacher gave **each** child a piece of paper and asked them to draw a picture.

earth

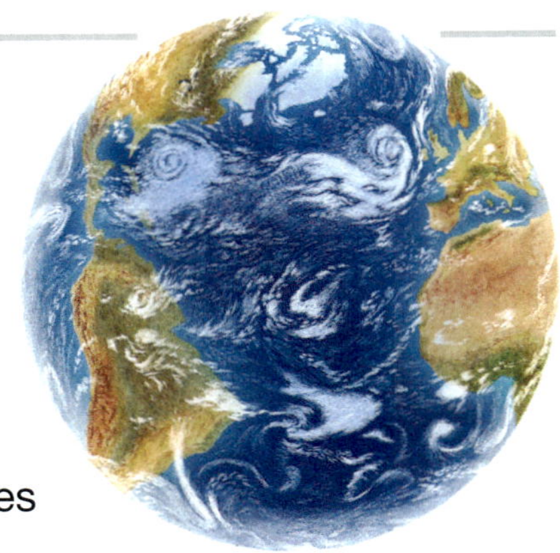

1 We all live on a planet called **Earth**. Our **Earth** moves around the Sun.
2 The ground that plants grow in is also called **earth**. In spring we dig the **earth** and plant seeds in it.

eagle

An **eagle** is a large bird with a sharp, curved beak. **Eagles** catch and eat small animals and other birds.

earthquake

An **earthquake** happens when part of the ground suddenly begins to shake. **Earthquakes** sometimes make buildings fall down.

ear

People and animals hear with their **ears**. You have an **ear** on each side of your head. Elephants have big **ears**.

east

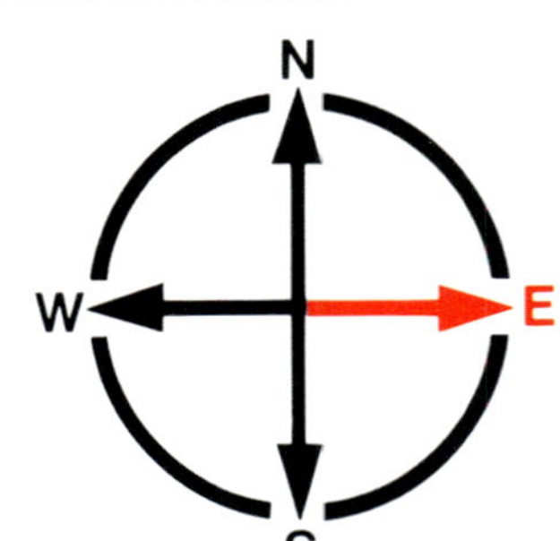

East is where the Sun comes up in the morning. The opposite direction is **west**.

easy (easier, easiest)

If something is **easy** to do, it is simple and it can be done without working very hard. This puzzle is very **easy**.

eat (eating, ate, eaten)

When you **eat**, you put food in your mouth and it goes down into your stomach.

echo (echoes)

An **echo** is the sound that comes back to you when you shout in a place like a cave.

edge

An **edge** is the end or side of something. Please don't put that glass so near the **edge** of the table.

egg

Birds, fish, reptiles and some other animals lay **eggs**. The young of these animals live inside **eggs** until they are ready to hatch. Hens lay **eggs** with hard shells which we use as food.

elbow

Your **elbows** are the parts in the middle of your arms where they bend.

electricity

Electricity is a kind of power that travels along wires. It makes heat and light, and it makes things like televisions and computers work.

elephant

An **elephant** is a very big, grey animal. Its long nose is called a trunk and it has two long teeth called tusks.

emerald

An **emerald** is a green jewel that is worth a lot of money.

empty (emptier, emptiest)

If something is **empty**, it has nothing or nobody inside. This bottle is **empty**. Who drank all the orange juice?

end

1 The **end** of something is the last part or the finish. You hold one **end** of the ladder and I'll hold the other. I'm almost at the **end** of my book.
2 (ending, ended) To **end** means to finish. What time does this film **end**?

energy

Energy makes things move and engines work. Electricity is one kind of **energy**. You use your own **energy** when you run or jump.

engine

An **engine** is a machine that makes things like cars and aeroplanes move.

Word play
E is a very useful letter. An **e** at the end of a word changes the sound of the vowel (a, e, i, o, u) that comes earlier in the word.

not + e = note

What new words can you make by adding an **e** to the end of these words?

plan

hop cub

kit bar

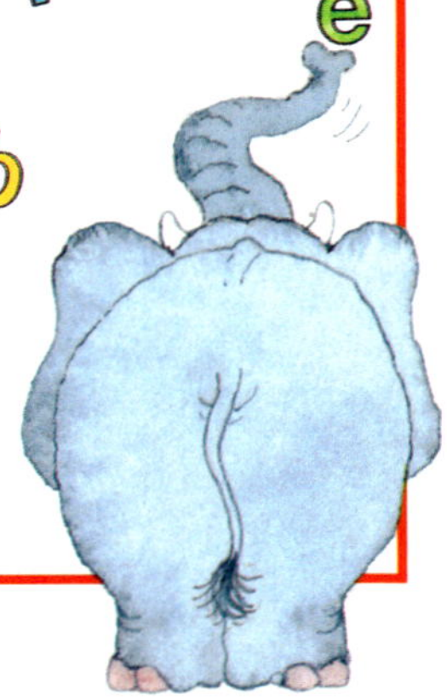

Answers on page 176.

enjoy (enjoying, enjoyed)

When you **enjoy** yourself, you feel happy about what you are doing. Did you **enjoy** yourself at the birthday party?

enormous

If something is **enormous**, it is very big. An elephant is an **enormous** animal.

enough

If you have **enough**, you have as much as you need or want. Have you had **enough** to eat?

enter (entering, entered)

When you **enter** a room or a building, you go in. The man **entered** the shop.

envelope

An **envelope** is a thing made of paper which covers a letter when you send it. You stick stamps on an **envelope**.

environment

The **environment** is everything around us, like the air that we breathe and the water that we drink. Some animals and plants will disappear for ever if we don't do more to protect the **environment**.

equal

1 If two things are **equal**, they are the same size or number. We have **equal** numbers of apples and oranges.
2 (equalling, equalled) If one thing **equals** another thing, they are the same size or the same number. Two plus two **equals** four.

escape (escaping, escaped)

When you **escape**, you get free or you get away from somebody or something. My hamster has **escaped** from its cage.

even

An **even** number is any number that ends in 2, 4, 6, 8 or 0. These numbers can be divided by 2 and leave nothing over. The opposite of **even** is odd.

evening

The **evening** is the part of the day between afternoon and night. The Sun goes down in the **evening**.

ever

1 Ever means at any time. Have you **ever** flown in an aeroplane?
2 Ever also means for all time. They lived happily **ever** after.

evil

Evil means very, very bad. In the story, the country was ruled by an **evil** king who treated his people very badly.

excellent

Something that is **excellent** is very, very good. We went to see an **excellent** film last Saturday.

except

Except means leaving out somebody or something. All the puppies are brown **except** the little one, which is white.

excited

If you are **excited**, you are so happy that you cannot keep quiet or stand still. We're getting very **excited** about our holiday.

excuse

An **excuse** is what you say to explain why you did or did not do something. What is your **excuse** for being so late?

exercise

1 Exercise is something, like running or jumping, that you do to keep your body strong and well. We do lots of different **exercises** in the gym at school.
2 An **exercise** is a small piece of work that you do to help you learn something. Finish **exercise** 3 before you go out to play.

exit

An **exit** is the way out of a building. Can you show me where the **exit** is, please?

expect (expecting, expected)

If you **expect** something, you think that it will happen. I'm **expecting** my friend to telephone today.

expensive

Something that is **expensive** costs a lot of money to buy. New bikes are very **expensive**.

explain (explaining, explained)

When you **explain** something, you tell people about it so that they can understand. Can you **explain** to me how this machine works?

explode (exploding, exploded)

When something **explodes**, it breaks into pieces with a loud noise. The fireworks **exploded** in the sky.

explore (exploring, explored)

When you **explore**, you look carefully around a place you have never seen before.

On holiday, the children **explored** the wood to see what they could find.

extra

Extra means more than usual. Emily asked for an **extra** slice of cake.

eye

Your **eyes** are the parts of your face that you use for seeing.

Another word that sounds like **eye** is **I**.

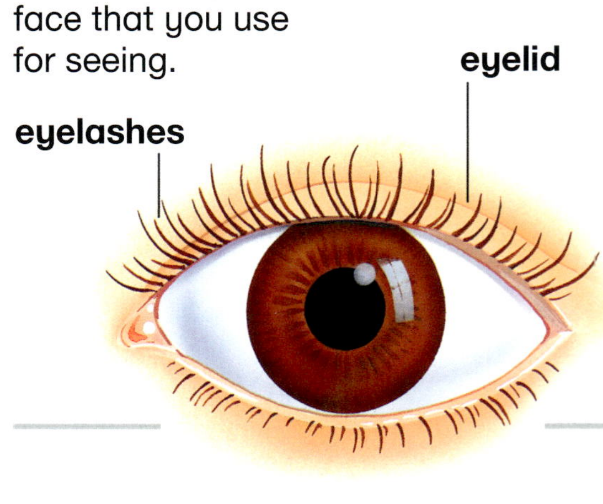

face

Your **face** is the front part of your head. Your eyes, nose and mouth are on your **face**.

fact

A **fact** is something that is true. It is a **fact** that the world is round.

factory (factories)

A **factory** is a building where people use machines to make things. Cars are made in **factories**.

fair

1 Something that is **fair** seems right. You must be **fair** – if you give Emma a sweet, you should give one to Elliot as well.
2 **Fair** hair has a light colour.
3 A **fair** is a place outside where you can have fun by riding on big machines with seats and playing games to win prizes. I won a doll at the **fair**.

fairy (fairies)

A **fairy** is a very small person that you can read about in stories. **Fairies** have magic powers and they can fly.

fall (falling, fell, fallen)

When somebody or something **falls**, it suddenly comes down to the ground. She **fell** over in the playground.

false

If something is **false**, it is not true or not real. The man gave a **false** name to the police instead of his real name.

family (families)

A **family** is a group of people made up of parents, grandparents and children. If you have aunts, uncles and cousins, they are also part of your **family**.

famous

A **famous** person or thing is well known. The Eiffel Tower is a **famous** tower in France.

far (farther, farthest)

Far means a long way. I can't walk to school – it's too **far**.

farm

A **farm** is a place where people keep animals or grow crops for food. The person who looks after a **farm** is called a **farmer**.

farther Look at **far**.

fast

Something that is **fast** can move quickly. I can run **faster** than my brother.

fat

1 (fatter, fattest) A person or an animal that is **fat** has a big, round body. Our dog is very **fat** because she eats a lot.
2 Fat is something like oil or butter that you can use in cooking.

father

A **father** is a man who has a child.

fault

If something bad is your **fault**, you made it happen. It isn't my **fault** that we're late.

favourite

Your **favourite** is the one that you like best. What is your **favourite** colour?

fear

Fear is the feeling of being afraid. Many animals have a **fear** of water.

feather

Birds have **feathers** all over their bodies. **Feathers** are very light.

feed (feeding, fed)

If you **feed** an animal, you give food to it.

We like **feeding** the ducks in the park.

feel (feeling, felt)

1 When you **feel** something, you touch it to find out what it is like. **Feel** this wool – it's really soft.
2 When you **feel** ill, hot or tired, you are that way at the moment. I **felt** sad when my cat ran away.

feet Look at **foot**.

fell Look at **fall**.

felt Look at **feel**.

female

A **female** person or animal belongs to the sex that can have babies.

Women and girls are **female**.

fence

A **fence** is a thing like a wall that is usually made of wood or wire. People put **fences** around gardens and fields.

fetch (fetches, fetching, fetched)

If you **fetch** somebody or something, you go and get it and bring it back. Could you **fetch** my coat from the hall, please?

few

Few means not many. We invited a lot of friends to the party but only a **few** of them could come.

field

A **field** is a piece of land where farmers grow crops or keep animals. Many **fields** have fences or hedges around them.

fierce

An animal that is **fierce** is angry and dangerous. Tigers can be **fierce**.

fight (fighting, fought)

When people or animals **fight**, they try to hurt each other.

fill (filling, filled)

When you **fill** something, you put as much into it as you can.

Dean is **filling** the glass with juice.

film

1 A **film** is a story in moving pictures that you watch on a screen.
2 A **film** is also a roll of thin plastic that you put in a camera for taking photographs.

find (finding, found)

When you **find** something, you see what you were looking for. I lost my watch but my friend **found** it in the playground.

fine

Fine means very good. I hope the weather stays **fine** for our picnic. I had a cold last week, but I feel **fine** now.

finger

Your **fingers** are the five long, thin parts at the end of your hand.

finish (finishes, finishing, finished)

When you **finish** something, you come to the end of it. When I've **finished** my painting, I'll show it to you.

fire

Fire is the hot, bright light that comes from things that are burning.

fire-fighter

A **fire-fighter** is a person who has the job of putting out fires. A group of **fire-fighters** who work together is called a **fire brigade**. They travel to fires in a big truck called a **fire engine**.

fireworks

Fireworks are things that send out showers of coloured lights when somebody sets fire to them. **Fireworks** often make a loud noise at the same time.

firm

Something that is **firm** is not soft or it does not move or change shape much when you touch it. Bananas are **firm** when they are green but they get softer when they are ripe.

first

First means at the front or at the beginning. I won the race – I came **first**. January is the **first** month of the year.

fish (fish or fishes)

A **fish** is an animal that lives under water. A **fish** has fins and a tail to help it swim about. Its body is covered in lots of small parts called scales.

fist

A **fist** is a hand that is closed tightly. John knocked on the door with his **fist**.

fit

1 (fitting, fitted) If something **fits**, it is the right size and shape.
These shoes don't **fit** Rosa any more. They're too small.
2 (fitter, fittest) If you are **fit**, you are strong and healthy.
My dad does exercises to keep himself **fit**.

fix (fixing, fixed)

1 If you **fix** something that is broken, you make it useful again. Katie is trying to **fix** my bike.
2 If you **fix** something to another thing, you join the two things together. My mum **fixed** the shelf to the wall.

flag

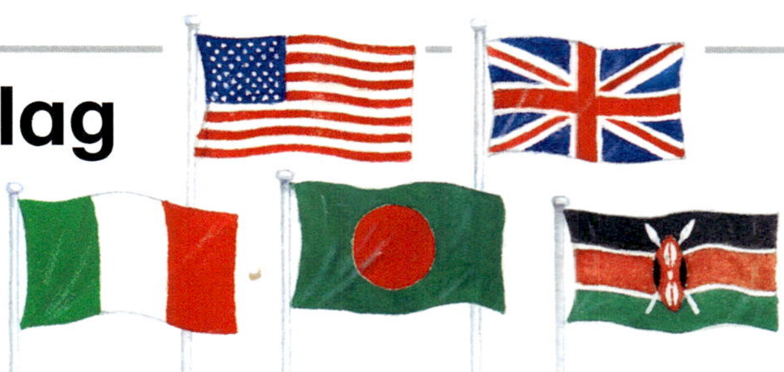

A **flag** is a piece of cloth with a coloured pattern on it, on the end of a long pole. Every country has its own **flag**.

flame

A **flame** is a hot, bright light that you see when something is burning.

flap (flapping, flapped)

When a bird **flaps** its wings, it moves them quickly up and down.

flash (flashes)

A **flash** is a bright light that comes and goes very quickly. We saw a **flash** of lightning in the sky.

flat

1 (flatter, flattest) Something that is **flat** is smooth and has no parts that are higher than the rest. A table has a **flat** top. I need somewhere **flat** to do my puzzle.
2 A **flat** is a group of rooms for living in. A **flat** is part of a larger building.

flavour

The **flavour** of food or drink is what it tastes like. Which **flavour** ice cream do you like best – chocolate or strawberry?

flew Look at **fly**.

Word play
How many words beginning with **f** can you make from these letters? You can use each letter as many times as you want.

Answers on page 176.

Flowers

crocus

carnation

sunflower

poppy

daffodil

tulip

lily

violet

Flying seeds
Some flower **seeds** are carried by the wind.

rose

flies Look at **fly**.

float
(floating, floated)

1 When something **floats** in a liquid, it stays on the top.
2 When something **floats** in air, it moves along gently in the air without falling. I let go of the balloon and it **floated** away.

flood

A **flood** happens when a lot of water covers a place that is usually dry. **Floods** usually happen when there has been a lot of rain.

floor

A **floor** is the flat part of a room that you walk on. Some children had to sit on the **floor** because there were not enough chairs.

flour

Flour is a white or brown powder that is made from wheat. We use **flour** to make bread and cakes.

Another word that sounds like **flour** is **flower**.

flow (flowing, flowed)

When a liquid **flows**, it moves along. The river **flows** into the sea.

flower

A **flower** is the pretty, coloured part of a plant. We gave Jenny some **flowers** on her birthday.

Another word that sounds like **flower** is **flour**.

fly

1 (flies, flying, flew, flown) When a bird, an insect or an aircraft **flies**, it moves through the air.
2 (flies) A **fly** is a small insect with wings.

foal

A **foal** is a young horse. The **foal** was born last spring.

fog

Fog is thick, cloudy air near the ground. It is difficult to see through **fog**.

fold (folding, folded)

If you **fold** something, you bend one part so that it covers another.

Tom is **folding** up his clothes before he puts them away.

follow (following, followed)

If you **follow** something or somebody, you go behind them. The dog **followed** me along the street.

food

Food is everything that people and animals eat. We eat **food** to stay alive and to grow.

foot (feet)

Your **foot** is the part at the end of your leg. You stand on your **feet**.

football

Football is a game for two teams who kick a ball and try to score goals.

foreign

A person or thing that is **foreign** comes from another country.

forest

A **forest** is a place where there are a lot of trees growing together. A lot of different birds and animals live in the **forest**.

forget (forgetting, forgot, forgotten)

When you **forget** something, you do not remember it. I have **forgotten** where I put my book. Have you seen it? I **forgot** to send Ben a card on his birthday.

fork

A **fork** is a tool with long pointed parts at one end. You use a small **fork** for putting food in your mouth. Big **forks** are used for digging the ground.

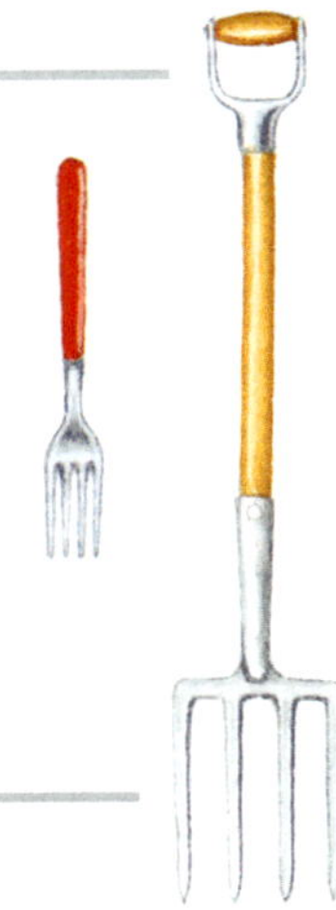

forwards

Forwards means towards what is in front. The car started to move **forwards**. The rope was swinging backwards and **forwards**.

fossil

A **fossil** is a dead animal or plant that has turned to stone after it has been in the ground for a long time.

fought Look at **fight**.

found Look at **find**.

Some words, such as **phone**, sound as if they begin with **f**, but you will find them in the dictionary under **ph**.

fox

A **fox** is a wild animal with red-brown fur and a long, thick tail.

frame

A **frame** is the wooden or metal part around something like a picture or a window.

free

1 If something is **free**, you do not have to pay for it. We got **free** tickets for the play because my dad works in the theatre.
2 If a person or an animal is **free**, they can go where they want and do what they want. I opened the cage and set the bird **free**.

freeze (freezing, froze, frozen)

1 When water **freezes**, it becomes ice.
2 If you are **freezing**, you are very cold. Could you close the window, please? I'm **freezing**.

fresh

1 Food that is **fresh** is not old or bad.
2 Fresh water is water that is not salty. Rivers and most lakes have **fresh** water in them.
3 Fresh air is air that is clean and good to breathe.

fridge

A **fridge** is a big metal box where you can put food to keep it cold and fresh.

fried Look at **fry**.

friend

A **friend** is somebody you know well and like a lot. Katie is my best **friend**.

friendly (friendlier, friendliest)

A **friendly** person is kind and helpful.

frighten (frightening, frightened)

If you **frighten** somebody, you make them afraid. My little brother is **frightened** of the dark.

frog

A **frog** is a small animal that lives in and near water. **Frogs** have strong back legs that help them to jump and swim.

front

The **front** of something is the part that you usually see first. Harry's book has a picture of a panda on the **front**.

frost

When there is a **frost**, the ground is covered in ice like white powder.

frown (frowning, frowned)

When you **frown**, you make a face to show that you are worried or angry, or that you are thinking hard.

froze Look at **freeze**.

frozen Look at **freeze**.

fruit

Fruit is a part of a plant that has the seeds in it. Apples, oranges and grapes are different kinds of **fruit** that we eat.

fry (frying, fried)

If you **fry** food, you cook it in a pan in hot oil.

full

Something that is **full** has no space for anything more. Charlotte's glass is **full**.

fun

When you have **fun**, you enjoy yourself. We all had a lot of **fun** at the birthday party.

funny (funnier, funniest)

1 Something that is **funny** makes you laugh or smile. My friend told me a **funny** joke.
2 Funny also means strange. The machine is making a **funny** noise.

fur

Fur is the soft, thick hair that covers the skin of many animals. Cats, dogs and bears are covered in **fur**.

furniture

Furniture is things like tables, chairs and beds that people have in their homes.

furry (furrier, furriest)

Something that is **furry** is covered in fur. A bear is a **furry** animal.

future

The **future** is the time that has not happened yet. In the **future**, people may go to the Moon on holiday.

Fruit

△ Some fruits have seeds called **pips** inside a **core.**

△ Some fruits have a **stone** in the middle. The **seed** is inside this stone.

△ Many fruits have lots of **pips** in the juicy inside part called the **flesh.**

Plant a tree
You can try growing your own fruit tree by planting some pips, seeds or a stone.

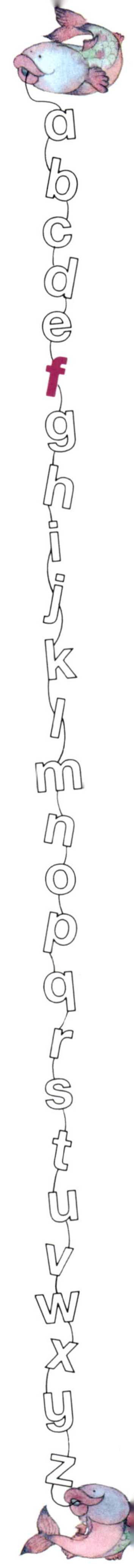

gallop (galloping, galloped)

When a horse **gallops**, it runs very fast. The horse is **galloping** around the field.

game

A **game** is a way of playing that has special rules. Tennis and football are **games** that you play with a ball. Snap is a **game** that you play with cards.

gap

A **gap** is a space between two things. I have a **gap** where my tooth has fallen out.

garage

1 A **garage** is a building where people keep their cars.
2 A **garage** is also a place that sells petrol or where people mend cars.

garden

A **garden** is a piece of land near a house, where people grow flowers and vegetables.

gas (gases)

A **gas** is something like air that does not have a shape. The air we breathe is made of different **gases** mixed together. We burn another kind of **gas** to cook our food and heat our homes.

gate

A **gate** is a kind of door in a wall or a fence. Close the **gate** to the field so that the horse can't get out.

gave Look at **give**.

geese Look at **goose**.

gentle

If you are **gentle**, you are quiet and kind and you do things carefully. Be **gentle** with the baby.

gerbil

A **gerbil** is a small, furry animal with long back legs. Some people keep **gerbils** in cages as pets.

Games

draughts
ludo
dice
board
counter
dominoes
noughts and crosses
skittles
card game
skipping
electronic game

ghost

A **ghost** is the shape of a dead person that some people say they have seen. Emma is dressed up as a **ghost**.

give

(giving, gave, given)

When you **give** something, you let another person have it. Clara **gave** Richard a present for his birthday.

giant

A **giant** is a very big person that you can read about in stories.

glad

If you are **glad**, you are happy. I'm **glad** you can come to my party.

gigantic

If something is **gigantic**, it is very big. I ate a **gigantic** pizza for lunch!

glass

1 Glass is a smooth, hard material that you can see through. Windows and car windscreens are made of **glass**.
2 (glasses) A **glass** is a kind of cup made of glass. May I have a **glass** of milk?

giggle (giggling, giggled)

If you **giggle**, you laugh in a silly way. The funny story made us all **giggle**.

glasses

People wear **glasses** over their eyes to help them see better. **Glasses** are made of a special kind of glass in a metal or plastic frame.

giraffe

A **giraffe** is a very tall wild animal that lives in Africa. It has long legs and a very long neck.

glove

People wear **gloves** to keep their hands warm or to protect them. **Gloves** have parts that cover each finger.

girl

A **girl** is a female child who will grow up to be a woman.

glue

Glue is a sticky liquid that you use for joining things together.

goal

1 A **goal** is the place where you have to make the ball go to score a point in games like football.
2 A **goal** is also a point that you score when a ball goes into a goal.

goat

A **goat** is an animal with rough hair. Some **goats** have horns. A young **goat** is called a kid.

gold

Gold is a shiny, yellow metal that people use to make rings, coins and other things.

good (better, best)

1 When something is **good**, people like it. That film was really **good**.
2 If you are **good**, you do as you are told.
3 If you are **good** at something, you can do it well. Are you **good** at spelling?
4 If something is **good** for you, it makes you healthy. Eating fresh fruit is **good** for you.

goose (geese)

A **goose** is a big bird with a long neck that swims well and lives near water. A young **goose** is called a gosling.

grab (grabbing, grabbed)

If you **grab** something, you take it quickly and roughly. The robber **grabbed** the money and ran away.

grandfather

Your **grandfather** is the father of your mother or father. My **grandfather** came to visit us last Saturday.

grandmother

Your **grandmother** is the mother of your mother or father. My **grandmother** gave me some money for my birthday.

grape

A **grape** is a small, round fruit that grows in bunches. **Grapes** are green or purple.

grapefruit

A **grapefruit** is a big, round, yellow fruit. **Grapefruits** are like oranges but they are not as sweet.

Grapefruits got their name because they grow in bunches, like huge grapes.

Word play
This ghost message is disappearing! Can you read it?

Well done

Answer on page 176.

grass (grasses)

Grass is a plant with thin, green leaves that covers fields, parks and gardens. Horses and cows eat **grass**.

great

1 Great means very good. We had a **great** time at the seaside.
2 Great also means very important and famous. The king was a **great** leader.
3 Great also means very big. There was a **great** crowd of people outside the theatre.

greedy (greedier, greediest)

A person who is **greedy** wants more of something than they really need. Don't be **greedy** – leave some cake for your brother.

grew Look at **grow**.

ground

The **ground** is what you walk on when you are outside. A bird landed on the **ground** near my feet.

group

A **group** is a number of people or things that are together in one place. A **group** of children stood outside the school gates.

grow (growing, grew, grown)

When something **grows**, it gets bigger and bigger. Animals and plants **grow**.

grown-up

A **grown-up** is a person who has finished growing. Parents are **grown-ups**.

guard (guarding, guarded)

To **guard** means to watch somebody or something all the time to make sure that nothing bad happens. Our neighbours have a big dog to **guard** their house.

guess (guesses, guessing, guessed)

When you **guess**, you try to give the answer to something without really knowing if it is right. Can you **guess** how many apples are in my bag?

guitar

A **guitar** is a musical instrument with strings that you play with your fingers.

gym

A **gym** is a room where people play games and do exercises. Our school has a big **gym**.

habit

A **habit** is something that you do often. Biting your nails is a bad **habit**.

hair

Hair is what grows on your head. Animals and people have **hair**.

half (halves)

A **half** is one of two pieces of something that are the same size. I had one **half** of the orange and my friend had the other **half**.

hall

A **hall** is the space inside a building that has doors leading to other rooms.

Hallowe'en

Hallowe'en is the thirty-first of October. Some people believe that witches and ghosts appear at **Hallowe'en**.

halves

Look at **half**.

hamburger

A **hamburger** is a round, flat piece of meat in a flat bread roll.

hammer

A **hammer** is a heavy tool that people use for hitting nails into wood or walls.

hamster

A **hamster** is a small, furry animal. They have large cheeks where they can store food. Some people keep **hamsters** as pets.

hand

Your **hands** are the parts of your body at the ends of your arms. A **hand** has four fingers and a thumb. We use our **hands** for picking things up and holding them.

handle

A **handle** is the part of something which you use to carry or hold it. Things like doors, mugs and scissors have **handles**.

hang (hanging, hung)

Something that is **hanging** is fixed at the top to something above it. The clothes are **hanging** out to dry.

happy (happier, happiest)

If you are **happy**, you feel good about something. You smile when you are **happy**.

hard

1 If something is **hard**, you cannot break or cut it easily, or shape it with your hands. Stone is **hard**.
2 Something that is **hard** is difficult. I can't do this puzzle. It's too **hard**.

hat

A **hat** is something you wear on your head.

hatch (hatches, hatching, hatched)

When a baby bird **hatches**, it breaks out of its egg. Three chicks **hatched** this morning.

hate (hating, hated)

If you **hate** something, you have a very strong feeling of not liking it.

hay

Hay is dry grass that is used for feeding animals.

head

1 Your **head** is the top part of your body that has your eyes, ears and mouth in it.
2 The **head** is also the leader. What's the name of the **head** teacher at your school?

heal (healing, healed)

When something like a cut **heals**, it gets well again. His broken leg **healed** quickly.

healthy (healthier, healthiest)

If you are **healthy**, you are not ill.

hear (hearing, heard)

When you **hear** sounds, you notice them with your ears.

Another word that sounds like **hear** is **here**.

heart

Your **heart** is inside your chest. It sends blood to all parts of your body.

heat

1 (heating, heated) If you **heat** something, you make it hot. David **heated** some milk in a saucepan.
2 Heat also means being warm or hot. Stand by the fire – the **heat** will soon dry your wet clothes.

heavy (heavier, heaviest)

Something that is **heavy** is difficult to lift or move. These books are too **heavy** for Tom to pick up.

hedge

A **hedge** is a line of bushes or small trees that make a kind of wall.

heel

1 Your **heel** is the back part of your foot.
2 A **heel** is also the back part of a shoe.

height

The **height** of something or somebody is how tall they are.

What **height** are you?

held Look at **hold**.

helicopter

A **helicopter** is an aircraft without wings. It has long sharp parts, called blades, which turn around on top.

helmet

A **helmet** is a hard hat that people wear to protect their heads. Gemmel is wearing a bicycle **helmet**.

help (helping, helped)

If you **help** somebody, you do something useful for them. I **helped** my teacher by carrying the books for her.

hen

A **hen** is a female chicken. **Hens** lay eggs.

hide (hiding, hid, hidden)

1 When you **hide**, you go into a place where people cannot see you.

Harry is **hiding** from his friends.

2 When you **hide** something, you put it where people cannot see it. I **hid** my sister's shoes under the bed.

high

Something that is **high** goes up a long way. This wall is very **high**. Mount Everest is the **highest** mountain in the world.

hill

A **hill** is a piece of ground that is higher than the land around it. We climbed to the top of the **hill**.

hippo

A **hippo** is a big wild animal that lives in and near rivers and lakes in hot countries. **Hippo** is short for **hippopotamus**.

Hippopotamus is made from two Greek words that mean 'river horse'.

Word play
Play this dictionary game with a friend. Open the dictionary at any page and read out the first and last words on that page. Your friend must try to guess any of the other words on the page!

hit (hitting, hit)

If you **hit** somebody or something, you touch it very hard. I tried to **hit** the ball with the bat.

hive

A **hive** is a box for keeping bees in. Bees make honey inside **hives**.

hobby (hobbies)

A **hobby** is something that you enjoy doing when you have free time. My **hobbies** are swimming, reading and collecting stamps.

hold (holding, held)

1 When you **hold** something, you have it in your hand. Bobby is **holding** a bunch of flowers.

2 Hold also means to have something inside. This bottle **holds** a litre of water.

hole

A **hole** is an empty space or gap. Joe has a **hole** in his sock.

Another word that sounds like **hole** is **whole**.

holiday (holidays)

A **holiday** is a time when you do not go to work or school. What did you do in the summer **holidays**?

hollow

Something that is **hollow** has an empty space inside. A drum is **hollow**.

home

Your **home** is the place where you live.

honest *say *onnist*

If somebody is **honest**, they always tell the truth. If you are **honest**, people will trust you.

honey

Honey is a thick, sweet food that bees make.

hop (hopping, hopped)

1 When you **hop**, you jump on one foot.
2 When an animal **hops**, it moves in small jumps. Kangaroos, frogs and some other animals **hop**.

hope (hoping, hoped)

If you **hope** that something will happen, you want it to happen and you think that it will. I **hope** you will be able to come to my party.

horn

A **horn** is a hard, pointed thing that grows out of the heads of some animals, like goats, bulls and some sheep.

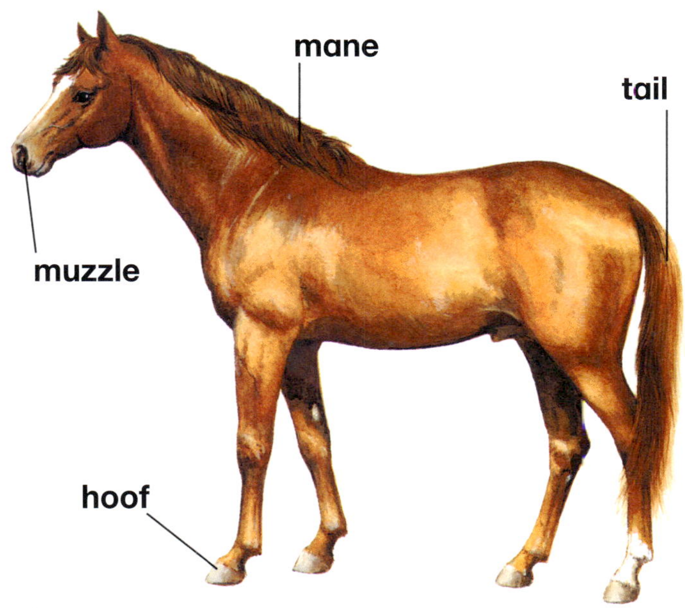

horse

A **horse** is an animal with a long tail and long hair, called a mane, on its neck. People ride **horses** and use them for pulling things like wagons. A young **horse** is called a foal.

hospital

A **hospital** is a large building where doctors and nurses look after people who are ill. We went to visit my aunt in **hospital**.

The human body

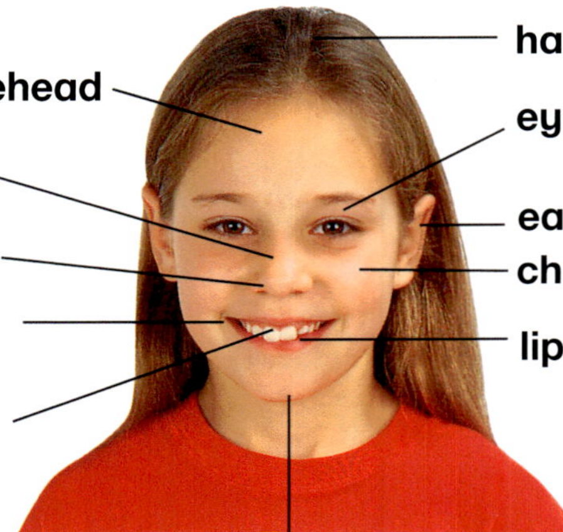

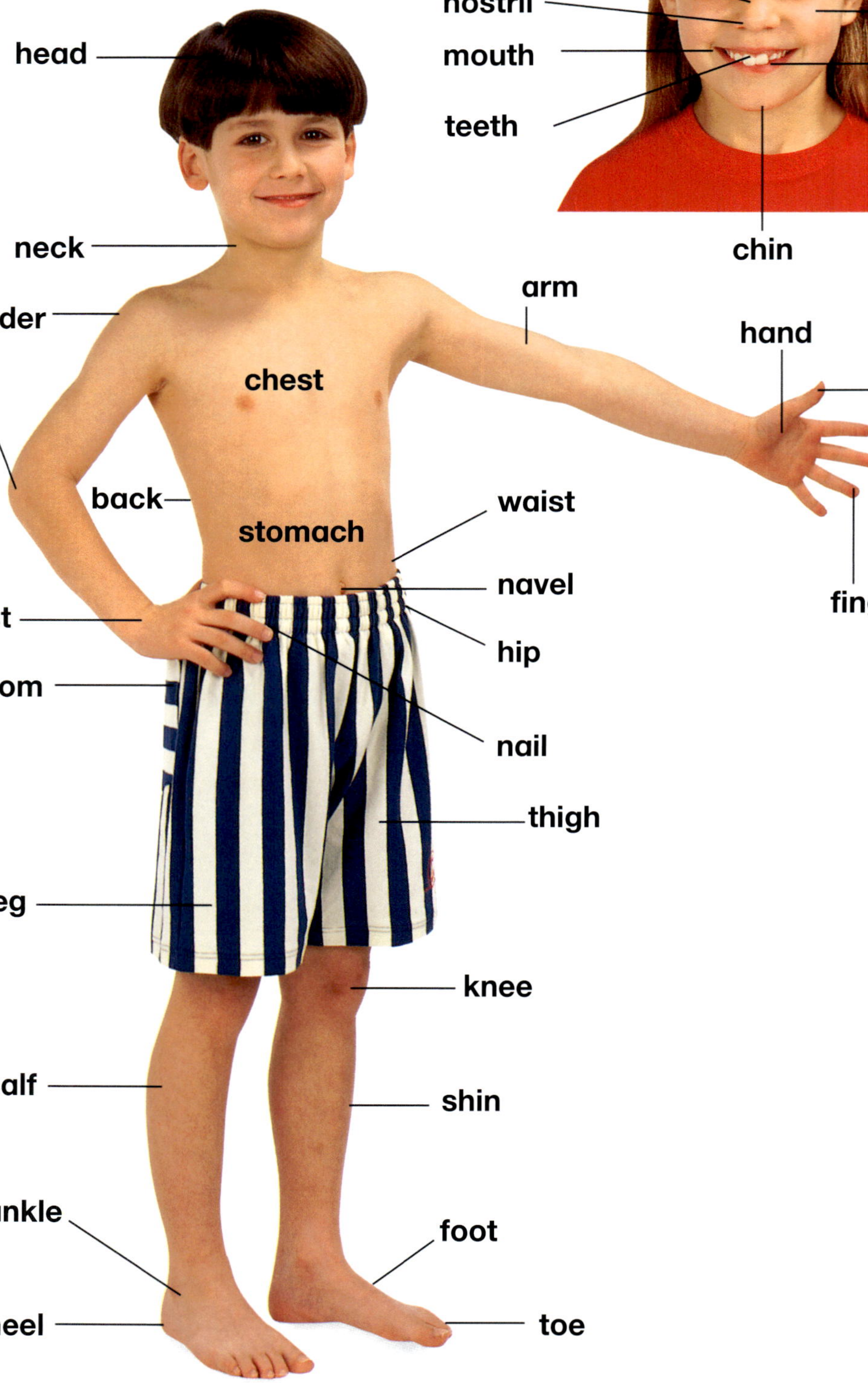

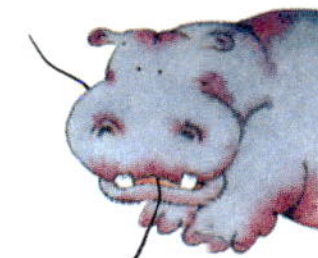

hot (hotter, hottest)

The Sun is **hot**, and so is fire. **Hot** things can burn you. An oven gets very **hot** inside.

hotel

A **hotel** is a building with a lot of bedrooms, where people can stay when they are away from home.

hour

An **hour** is a time of 60 minutes. There are 24 **hours** in a day.

Another word that sounds like **hour** is **our**.

house

A **house** is a building where people live. How many rooms does your **house** have?

huge

If something is **huge**, it is very big.

human

A **human** is a person.

hump

A **hump** is a big round part on a camel's back. Camels have one or two **humps**.

hung Look at **hang**.

hungry (hungrier, hungriest)

When you are **hungry**, you feel that you want to eat something.

hunt (hunting, hunted)

1 When animals **hunt**, they chase other animals and kill them for food.
2 When you **hunt** for something, you look carefully for it. I **hunted** all over the house for my book.

hurry (hurries, hurrying, hurried)

When you **hurry**, you go somewhere or do something as quickly as you can. If you don't **hurry** up, you will be late for school.

hurt (hurting, hurt)

If you **hurt** a part of your body or if it **hurts**, it gives you pain.

I fell over and **hurt** my leg.

husband

A woman's **husband** is the man she is married to.

hut

A **hut** is a small, simple building. **Huts** usually have only one room inside. Many **huts** are made of wood or grass.

a b c d e f g **h** i j k l m n o p q r s t u v w x y z

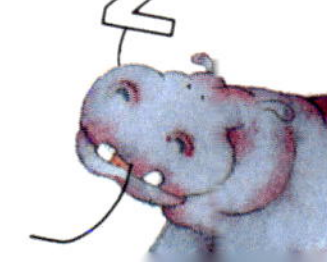

ice

Ice is water that has become hard because it is very cold.

ice cream

Ice cream is a sweet, frozen food.

icicle

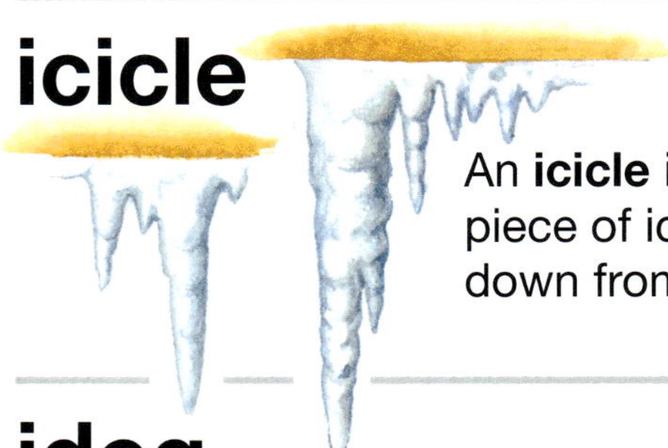

An **icicle** is a long piece of ice hanging down from something.

idea

When you have an **idea**, you think of something. Do you have any good **ideas** for games we can play at the party?

igloo

An **igloo** is a house made of blocks of snow or ice.

ill

When you are **ill**, you are not well. My sister is staying in bed today because she's **ill**.

imagine (imagining, imagined)

When you **imagine** something, you have a picture of it in your mind. Close your eyes and **imagine** you are on the beach.

immediately

If you do something **immediately**, you do it now, without waiting. We must leave **immediately** or we'll miss our train.

important

1 Something that is **important** matters a lot. It is **important** to look both ways before you cross the road.
2 If somebody is **important**, they have a lot of power. The President of the United States is a very **important** person.

impossible

If you say something is **impossible**, it cannot be done. It's **impossible** for a person to walk on the ceiling.

information

Information is the facts about something. This dictionary gives you **information** about words and how to spell them.

ink

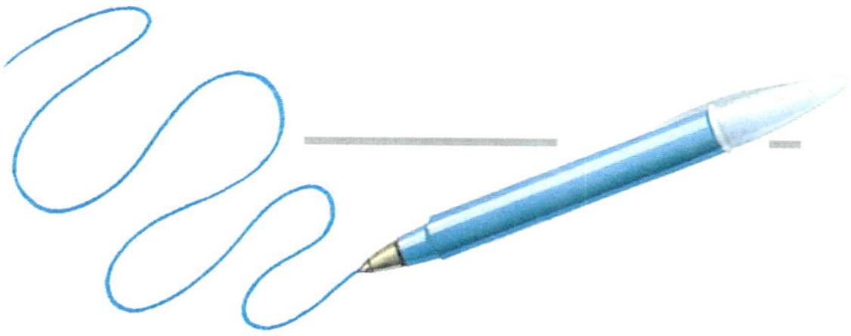

Ink is the coloured liquid that is used for writing or printing. The words on this page were printed with **ink**.

insect

An **insect** is a very small creature with six legs. Many **insects** have wings. Earwigs, grasshoppers and dragonflies are **insects**.

inside

If you are **inside** something, it is all around you. My fish is swimming around **inside** its bowl.

instead

Instead means in the place of something. I don't like tea – can I have water **instead**?

instrument

1 An **instrument** is something that is used for doing a special job. A telescope is an **instrument** that is used for looking at things that are far away.
2 A musical **instrument** is something that you play to make music. Guitars and pianos are musical **instruments**.

interesting

If something is **interesting**, you like it and want to find out more about it. Our school visit to the museum was very **interesting**.

invent (inventing, invented)

If you **invent** something, you make something that has never been made or thought of before. Thomas Edison was a famous **inventor**. He **invented** the light bulb.

invisible

If something is **invisible**, it cannot be seen.

invite (inviting, invited)

If you **invite** somebody, you ask them to come somewhere to do something. My brother has **invited** ten friends to his birthday party. He has sent them all **invitations**.

iron

1 Iron is a strong, hard metal.
2 An **iron** is a tool which we use to make clothes smooth. **Irons** are flat on the bottom and they get very hot.

island *say *eye land*

An **island** is a piece of land with water all around it.

jacket

A **jacket** is a short coat.

jam

1 Jam is a sweet food made by cooking fruit with sugar.
2 (jamming, jammed) If something **jams**, it becomes difficult to move. The window won't open – it's **jammed**.

jar

A **jar** is a wide glass bottle. Jam and a lot of other foods come in **jars**.

jaw

Your **jaw** is the bone at the bottom of your face. You move your **jaw** when you eat and speak.

jeans

Jeans are trousers that are made of strong cotton cloth called denim.

jelly (jellies)

Jelly is a sweet food that you can see through.

jet

A **jet** is an aircraft that can fly very fast.

jewel

A **jewel** is a beautiful stone that is worth a lot of money. Diamonds, emeralds and rubies are **jewels**.

job

1 A **job** is something that you have to do. It's my brother's **job** to wash the dishes after dinner.
2 Somebody's **job** is the work that they do to get money.

jog (jogging, jogged)

To **jog** means to run slowly. My mum **jogs** around the park every morning.

Some words, such as **gentle**, sound as if they begin with **j**, but you will find them in the dictionary under **g**.

join (joining, joined)

1 If you **join** things, you put or fix them together.
2 If you **join** a group, you become part of it. I've **joined** a football team.

joke

A **joke** is something that you say or do to make people laugh.

journey (journeys)

When you go on a **journey**, you travel from one place to another. How long does your **journey** to school take?

juice

Juice is the liquid that comes from fruit. Would you like orange **juice** or grapefruit **juice** to drink?

jump (jumping, jumped)

When you **jump**, you move suddenly into the air.

jumper

A **jumper** is something that you wear. It covers your arms and the top part of your body to keep you warm. **Jumpers** are usually made of wool.

jungle

A **jungle** is a thick forest in a hot country.

junk

Junk is things that are old and not useful any more. This box is full of **junk**.

Word play
How many clothes words can you find by reading across and down in this word search box? Look at page 34 if you need any help.

x	i	s	p	d	e
f	b	c	a	p	s
j	e	a	n	s	o
u	l	r	t	h	c
p	t	f	s	o	k
g	l	o	v	e	t

Answers at the back!

kangaroo
(kangaroos)

A **kangaroo** is a wild animal that lives in Australia. It has strong back legs and moves by making long jumps.

A female **kangaroo** has a sort of bag at the front where she keeps her baby.

keep (keeping, kept)

1 If you **keep** something, you hold on to it and do not give it away. You can **keep** this book – I don't need it.
2 When you **keep** something in a place, you have it there. You must **keep** your money somewhere safe.
3 If you **keep** doing something, you do it many times. My little brother **keeps** following me around.
4 **Keep** also means to stay in the same way. **Keep** still while I take your photo.

kept
Look at **keep**.

ketchup

Ketchup is a kind of food made from tomatoes. I would like lots of **ketchup** on my hamburger.

kettle

You use a **kettle** for heating water. It has a lid, a handle and a pointed part, called a spout, for pouring.

key
(keys)

1 A **key** is a piece of metal that you turn to lock or unlock something.
2 The **keys** of a piano or a computer are the parts that you press with your fingers.

kick (kicking, kicked)

If you **kick** something, you hit it with your foot.

Harry has **kicked** the ball.

kid

1 A **kid** is a young goat.
2 People also sometimes call children **kids**.

kill (killing, killed)

To **kill** means to make somebody or something die.

kind

1 A **kind** person is nice to other people and ready to help them.
2 A **kind** is a group of things that are the same in some way. Kangaroos and elephants are two **kinds** of animal.

king

Some countries are ruled by a man called a **king**. The wife of a **king** is called a queen.

kingdom

A **kingdom** is a country that is ruled by a king or queen. The king was the richest man in the whole **kingdom**.

kiss (kisses, kissing, kissed)

When you **kiss** somebody, you touch them with your lips in a friendly way.

kit

A **kit** is a set of things. The driver took out her tool **kit** to fix the engine.

kitchen

A **kitchen** is a room where food is cooked.

kite

A **kite** is a toy that you fly in the wind at the end of a long piece of string. **Kites** are made of paper, plastic or cloth.

kitten

A **kitten** is a very young cat. Our cat has just had **kittens**.

knee *say *nee*

Your **knees** are the parts in the middle of your legs where they bend.

kneel *say *neel*

(kneeling, knelt)

When you **kneel**, you go down on your knees.

knew Look at **know**.

Another word that sounds like **knew** is **new**.

knife *say *nife* (knives)

A **knife** is a tool for cutting. It has a handle and a long sharp piece of metal called a blade.

knight

Long ago, a **knight** was a soldier who fought to protect a king or a queen.

Knights rode horses and many **knights** wore armour.

Another word that sounds like **knight** is **night**.

Word play

Put the words in each group in the order in which they come in the dictionary. If the first letter is the same, look at the second letter and so on.

1 key, car, wheel

2 puppy, powder, pretty

3 triangle, true, tractor

Answers at the back!

knit *say *nit*

(knitting, knitted)

When you **knit**, you use two long needles and wool to make clothes.

knock *say *nok* (knocking, knocked)

If you **knock** something, you hit it hard. Nadia **knocked** on the door.

knot

You make a **knot** when you twist and tie pieces of string or thread together.

Another word that sounds like **knot** is **not**.

know (knowing, knew, known)

1 If you **know** somebody, you have met them before. I **know** her because she is in my class.

2 If you **know** something, you have it in your mind. Everybody **knows** their own name.

Another word that sounds like **know** is **no**.

koala

A **koala** is an animal that looks like a small bear with thick, grey fur. It lives in trees and it is only found in Australia.

label

A **label** is a small note fixed to something. It may tell you what the thing is made of or who it belongs to.

lace

1 A **lace** is a thin string that you use to hold things together. Do up your **shoelaces**.
2 Lace is pretty cloth with a pattern of holes in it. The dress had a **lace** collar.

ladder

A **ladder** is a set of steps that you use for climbing up to a high place.

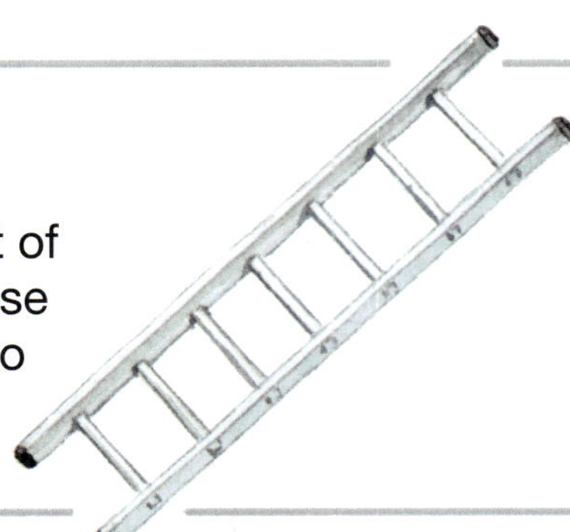

ladybird

A **ladybird** is a small, round beetle that can fly. **Ladybirds** are usually red with black spots.

laid

Look at **lay**.

lain

Look at **lie**.

lake

A **lake** is a lot of water with land all around it.

lamb

A **lamb** is a young sheep.

lamp

A **lamp** is something that gives out light in the dark.
I have a reading **lamp** by my bed.

land

1 Land is the part of the Earth that is not covered in water.
2 (landing, landed) When an aeroplane **lands**, it comes down from the air onto the ground. The aeroplane **landed** in a field.

language

Language is the words we use to speak, read and write to each other. There are many different **languages** in the world, such as English, French and Swahili.

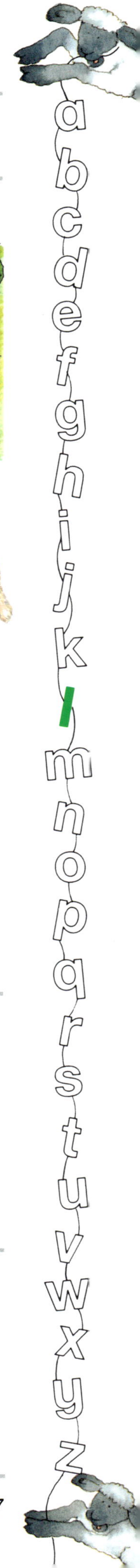

lap

Your **lap** is the top of your legs when you are sitting down.
My cat likes to sit on my **lap**.

large

Something that is **large** is big. Whales are very **large** animals.

last

1 When somebody or something is **last**, it is at the end or after all the others. Z is the **last** letter of the alphabet.
2 Last also means the one before this one. I went to bed late **last** night.

late

If you are **late**, you get to a place after the time you were supposed to. Sandra is often **late** for school.

laugh (laughing, laughed)

When you **laugh**, you make sounds that show that you think something is funny.

law

A **law** is a rule of a country that everybody must keep. Stealing is against the **law**.

lawn

A **lawn** is short grass around a house or another building.

lay (laying, laid)

1 When you **lay** something somewhere, you put it down carefully. Sam **laid** the sheet of paper on the teacher's desk.
2 When you **lay** a table, you put knives, forks and other things on it before you eat.
3 To **lay** also means to make an egg. Hens **lay** eggs.
4 Look at **lie**.

layer

A **layer** is something flat that lies under or over something else. The cake has a **layer** of cream in the middle.

lazy (lazier, laziest)

Somebody who is **lazy** does not want to do work or do very much. Don't be so **lazy**.

lead *rhymes with *seed*

1 (leading, led) When you **lead** somebody, you go in front to show them where to go.
2 A **lead** is a long chain, rope or piece of leather that you tie to a dog's collar so that you can take it for walks.

lead
*rhymes with *bed*

Lead is a very heavy, grey metal.

Another word that sounds like **lead** is **led**.

leader

A **leader** is the person who shows other people the way or who goes first.

leaf (leaves)

A **leaf** is one of the thin, flat parts that grow on plants.

Most **leaves** are green.

lean
(leaning, leant or leaned)

To **lean** means to rest against something or to bend in one direction.
Paul is **leaning** against a tree.

learn (learning, learnt or learned)

When you **learn** something, you find out about it or how to do it. My little sister is **learning** to swim.

leather

Leather is the skin of an animal. It is used to make things like shoes and gloves.

leave (leaving, left)

1 If you **leave**, you go away from a place. What time do you **leave** home to go to school in the mornings?
2 If you **leave** something somewhere, it stays where it is. Andrew **left** his bag at school so he had to go back to fetch it.

leaves Look at **leaf**.

led Look at **lead**.

left

1 Left is the opposite of right. Rosa has a puppet on her **left** hand.
2 Look at **leave**.

leg

1 Legs are the long parts of a person or an animal's body that are used for walking. People have two **legs**.
2 The **legs** of a chair or a table are the parts that it stands on.

lemon

A **lemon** is a yellow fruit with a sour taste.

length

The **length** of something is how long it is. The children are measuring the **length** of the table.

lesson

A **lesson** is a time when you learn something. I have a piano **lesson** every Tuesday afternoon.

letter

1 A **letter** is a message that you write on paper to another person.

Amy's friend has sent her a **letter**.

2 A **letter** is also one of the signs that we use for writing words. There are 26 **letters** in the English alphabet. D, H and Q are **letters**.

lettuce

A **lettuce** is a plant with large green leaves that you can eat in salads.

library (libraries)

A **library** is a place where a lot of books are kept. People can borrow books from a **library** and read them at home.

lick (licking, licked)

When you **lick** something, you move your tongue over it.

lid

A **lid** is the top part of a box, jar or other container. You lift the **lid** to open the container.

lie

1 A **lie** is something you say that you know is not true. Our teacher told us that we should never tell **lies**.
2 (lying, lay, lain) When you **lie** somewhere, you rest your body flat on something. Paulo is **lying** on the floor reading a book.

life (lives)

Life is the time when you are alive. I shall remember that day for the rest of my **life**.

lift

1 (lifting, lifted) If you **lift** something, you move it up.

Dean can only just **lift** the box of toys.

2 A **lift** is a thing like a big metal box that you stand in and that moves you up and down inside tall buildings.
3 If you get a **lift** with somebody, you travel with them in their car. My neighbour gave me a **lift** to school this morning.

light

1 Light is what comes from the Sun and from lamps. Without **light** you could not see anything.
2 Something that is **light** is not difficult to lift. A bag feels very **light** when there is nothing inside it.
3 Colours that are **light** are pale. I have a **light** blue dress.
4 (lighting, lit) When you **light** something, you make it burn. Jenny's dad **lit** the candles on the cake.

lighthouse

A **lighthouse** is a tower with a strong light on top, that helps ships to see dangerous rocks when it is dark.

lightning

Lightning is a flash of light that you see in the sky when there is a thunderstorm.

like

1 When something is **like** something else it is the same in some way. Carla is wearing a dress **like** mine.
2 (liking, liked) If you **like** something, it makes you happy. I **like** dancing and reading books.

likely

If something is **likely**, it will probably happen. It's very cold so it's **likely** to snow tonight.

line

1 A **line** is a long, thin mark. You can use a ruler to draw straight **lines** on paper.

2 A **line** is also a row of people or things. Our teacher asked us to stand in a **line**.

lion

A **lion** is a large wild cat. A female **lion** is called a lioness and a young **lion** is called a cub.

lip

Your **lips** are the soft, pink edges of your mouth.

liquid

A **liquid** is anything that is wet and that you can pour like water. Orange juice, milk and oil are all **liquids**.

list

A **list** is a group of words or names that are written down one after the other. We made a **list** so we could remember what to buy when we went shopping.

listen (listening, listened)

When you **listen**, you carefully try to hear something. Please **listen** to what I am saying. Do you ever **listen** to the radio?

lit Look at **light**.

little

1 Something that is **little** is small in size. The last toe on your foot is called your **little** toe.
2 A **little** means not very much. There is only a **little** juice left in Thomas's glass.

Word play
Can you find a word on this page that makes a different word if you spell it backwards?

Try to think of other words that do this. Here are some clues.

Answers on page 176.

live (living, lived)

1 To **live** means to be alive. Dinosaurs **lived** millions of years ago.
2 If you **live** somewhere, you have your home there. My aunt and uncle **live** in a little village in the country.

lives Look at **life**.

loaf (loaves)

A **loaf** is bread in a shape that can be cut into slices.

lock

1 A **lock** is something that is used to keep things like doors and drawers shut, so that you cannot open them without a key.
2 (locking, locked) When you **lock** something, you close it with a key. We **locked** all the doors and windows when we went out.

log

A **log** is a large, round piece of wood that has been cut from a tree.

long

Something that is **long** measures a lot from one end to the other.

The monkey has a **long** tail.

look (looking, looked)

1 If you **look** at somebody or something, you turn your eyes so that you can see it. **Look** at this picture.
2 If you **look** for something, you try to find it. I'm **looking** for my book. Have you seen it anywhere?

loose

If something is **loose**, it is not firmly fixed in one place. One of my teeth is **loose**.

lorry (lorries)

A **lorry** is a big machine for carrying heavy things by road.

lose (losing, lost)

1 When you **lose** something, you cannot find it. Mark has **lost** his glasses.
2 If you **lose** a game, you do not win it. Our team **lost** the match.

lost

If you are **lost**, you cannot find your way. Take this map so that you don't get **lost**.

loud

Something that is **loud** makes a lot of noise. The music is too **loud**. Please turn it down.

love (loving, loved)

If you **love** something or somebody, you like them very, very much. I **love** ice cream.

lovely

Something that is **lovely** is beautiful or very nice. We had a **lovely** holiday.

low

Something that is **low** is not high. The fence was so **low** that Josie could step over it.

lucky (luckier, luckiest)

If you are **lucky**, you have good things happen to you. Helen was very **lucky**. She didn't get hurt when she fell.

luggage

Luggage is all the bags that you carry your clothes and other things in when you travel.

lunch

Lunch is a meal that people eat in the middle of the day.

Dean is eating his **lunch**.

lying Look at **lie**.

machine

A **machine** is a thing with parts that move to do work or to make something. Computers and cars are both **machines**.

magazine

A **magazine** is a kind of thin book with pictures, photos and short stories in it. **Magazines** come out every week or month.

magic

Magic is a special power that is supposed to make strange and impossible things happen.

magician

A **magician** is a person who seems to make things happen by magic.

magnet

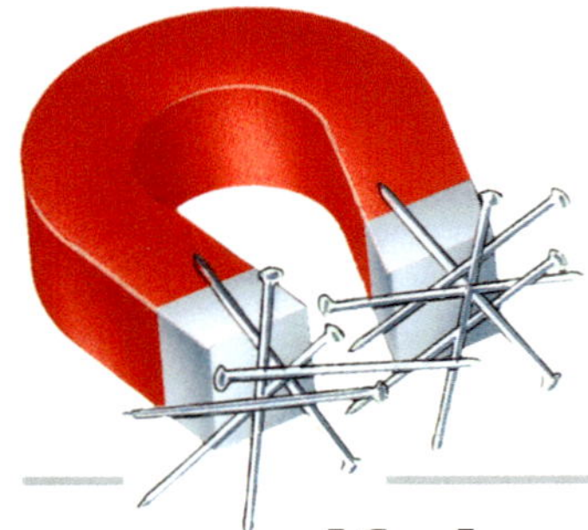

A **magnet** is a piece of metal that can pull other metal things towards it.

magnifying glass

A **magnifying glass** is a special piece of glass. When you look through it, things look bigger than they really are.

main

Main means most important. This is the **main** road through our town.

male

A **male** person or animal belongs to the sex that cannot have babies.

Boys and men are **male**.

mammal

A **mammal** is an animal that drinks milk from its mother's body when it is young. People, horses and whales are **mammals**.

man (men)

A **man** is a grown-up male person.

map

A **map** is a drawing that shows you what a place looks like from above. **Maps** show things like roads and rivers and they help you to find your way around a place.

mask

A **mask** is something that you can wear over your face to hide it or to protect it.

marble

1 Marble is a kind of very hard stone that is used to make things like statues and buildings.
2 A **marble** is a small glass ball that is used in games.

match

1 (matches) A **match** is a small, thin stick that makes fire when you rub it on something rough.
2 (matches) A **match** is also a game between two teams or players. We watched a football **match** on television.
3 (matches, matching, matched) If one thing **matches** another, it has the same colour, shape or pattern.

Katey's hat **matches** her scarf.

mark

A **mark** is a spot or a line on something that spoils it. Your dirty shoes have left a **mark** on the chair.

material

1 A **material** is anything that is used to make other things. Stone, wood and glass are **materials** that we use to build houses.
2 Material is cloth that we use to make clothes.

marmalade

Marmalade is a jam made from oranges or lemons.

marry (marries, marrying, married)

When a man and a woman **marry**, they become husband and wife.

matter (mattering, mattered)

If something **matters**, it is important. Ben has lost my ruler but it doesn't **matter** because I have got another one.

mattress (mattresses)

A **mattress** is the soft, thick part of a bed.

meal

When you have a **meal**, you sit down and eat something.

Breakfast, lunch and dinner are **meals**.

mean

1 (meaning, meant) If you ask what something **means**, you want somebody to explain it. What does this word **mean**?
2 (meaning, meant) If you **mean** to do something, you plan it and want to do it. I didn't **mean** to step on your foot.
3 Somebody who is **mean** does not like giving things or spending money.

measure
(measuring, measured)

When you **measure** something, you find out how big it is.

David is **measuring** his exercise book.

meat

Meat is part of an animal that we use as food. Beef is **meat** from a cow.

Another word that sounds like **meat** is **meet**.

medicine

Medicine is something that a doctor gives you when you are ill to make you feel better.

meet (meeting, met)

When you **meet** somebody, you go to the same place at the same time as them. **Meet** me outside school at four o'clock.

Another word that sounds like **meet** is **meat**.

melt (melting, melted)

When something **melts**, it changes into a liquid. The snowman **melted** in the warm sun.

memory

Memory is being able to remember things. If you have a good **memory**, you can remember lots of things.

men Look at **man**.

mend (mending, mended)

When you **mend** something that is broken, you make it useful again. I have broken my kite – can you **mend** it?

mention (mentioning, mentioned)

If you **mention** something, you say a little bit about it. Did Jo **mention** her party?

mess

A **mess** is when a lot of things are not where they belong. Your bedroom is in a terrible **mess** – please tidy it up!

message

A **message** is words that you send to somebody or that you ask another person to pass on to them. Tom isn't in. Would you like to leave a **message** for him?

met

Look at **meet**.

metal

Metal is a hard material that is used for making things like cars and aeroplanes. Silver and iron are different kinds of **metal**.

mice

Look at **mouse**.

microscope

A **microscope** is an instrument that makes very small things look much bigger. We looked at a drop of water under the **microscope**.

middle

The **middle** of something is the part that is not near the outside edges. There is a vase of flowers in the **middle** of the table.

midnight

Midnight is 12 o'clock at night.

milk

Milk is the white liquid that mothers make in their bodies to feed their babies. People drink the **milk** that cows make.

mind

1 Your **mind** is the part of you that you use for thinking and remembering.
2 If you do not **mind** something, you do not feel unhappy or angry about it. I don't **mind** if you play with my toys.
3 To **mind** also means to be careful of something. **Mind** the step!

mine

A **mine** is a place where people dig deep holes to find things like coal and gold.

minus

You use **minus** to talk about taking one number away from another. Four **minus** one is three.

minute *say *minnit*

A **minute** is a short time. There are 60 **minutes** in an hour.

mirror

A **mirror** is a piece of special glass that you can see yourself in.

miss (missing, missed)

1 If you **miss** something that you were trying to hit or catch, you do not hit or catch it. I tried to hit the ball but I **missed** it.
2 If you **miss** somebody, you are sad because you are not with them. I'll **miss** you when you go away.

mistake

A **mistake** is something you do that is wrong. You have made some spelling **mistakes** in this letter.

mix (mixing, mixed)

When you **mix** things, you stir them or put them together in some other way so that they make something new.

If you **mix** blue and red paint, you get purple.

model

A **model** is a small copy of something. Sue is building a **model** of a sailing boat.

moment

A **moment** is a very short time. Please wait for me – I will be ready in a **moment**.

money

Money is the coins and special pieces of paper, called bank-notes, that we use to pay for things.

monkey (monkeys)

A **monkey** is an animal with long arms and legs and a long tail. **Monkeys** live in hot countries. They are good at climbing and swinging from trees.

monster

A **monster** is a big, frightening creature that you can read about in stories.

month

A **month** is one of the 12 parts of a year. January is the first **month** of the year.

Moon

The **Moon** is a small planet that travels around the Earth once every four weeks. You can often see it in the sky at night.

morning

The **morning** is the early part of the day, before 12 o'clock.

moth

A **moth** is an insect with big wings. **Moths** look like butterflies but they usually fly around at night.

mother

A **mother** is a woman who has a child.

motorbike

A **motorbike** is a kind of big, heavy bicycle with an engine.

motorway

A **motorway** is a wide road where cars can move along fast.

mountain

A **mountain** is a very high hill. The highest **mountain** in the world is Mount Everest.

mouse (mice)

A **mouse** is a small, furry animal with a long tail and sharp teeth.

mouth

Your **mouth** is the part of your face that you open and close to talk and eat.

Word play

Can you read this?

What keys are furry? Monkeys!

Answers at the back!

Now try writing your own name so you can read it in a mirror.

Musical instruments

▽ You blow into the **mouthpiece** and press the **buttons** to play a **trumpet**.

drum

maracas

recorder

▷ You move the **bow** across the **strings** of the **violin** to play it.

xylophone

cymbals

◁ You blow across the hole at the top of a **flute** and press the buttons with your fingers.

▽ A **piano** has **keys** that you press to make sounds.

triangle

tambourine

move (moving, moved)

To **move** means to go from one place to another. Don't **move** – I want to take your photograph.

mud

Mud is soft, wet earth. When we came home from playing in the field, we were covered in **mud**.

mug

A **mug** is a big cup with straight sides. I drink my tea from a big, red **mug**.

multiply (multiplies, multiplying, multiplied)

When you **multiply** numbers, you do a sum with them to make a bigger number.

Two **multiplied** by four is eight.

muscle *say *mussel*

Your **muscles** are the stretchy parts under your skin. They get tight and loose to help you move.

museum

A **museum** is a building where a lot of interesting things are on show for people to look at. We saw a model of a dinosaur in the **museum**.

mushroom

A **mushroom** is a small plant without leaves, shaped like an umbrella. People eat some kinds of **mushrooms**.

music

Music is sounds that come from somebody singing or from a **musical instrument**, like a piano or a guitar. We learn a lot of songs in **music** lessons at school.

musician

A person who makes music is called a **musician**.

mystery (mysteries)

A **mystery** is something strange that has happened, that people cannot explain.

nail

1 Your **nails** are the hard, shiny parts that cover the ends of your fingers and toes.
2 A **nail** is also a short piece of metal with a point at one end. You hit a **nail** with a hammer to fix one thing to another.

name

A **name** is what you call somebody or something. My friends' **names** are David and Rosa.

narrow

Something that is **narrow** has two sides that are not far apart. The door of our house is very **narrow**.

nasty (nastier, nastiest)

Something or somebody that is **nasty** is not nice or kind. What a **nasty** smell!

natural

Something that is **natural** has not been made by people. Wood is a **natural** material, but plastic is not.

nature

1 Nature is everything in the world that was not made by people. We should do more to protect **nature**, not damage it.
2 A person or an animal's **nature** is what they are really like. Samantha is a nice girl – she has a kind **nature**.

naughty (naughtier, naughtiest)

A child who is **naughty** behaves badly.

near

Something that is **near** is not far away. I like sitting **near** the window.

nearly

Nearly means not quite. Sapphire is **nearly** as tall as Bobby.

neat

Neat means tidy. Fold your clothes and put them in a **neat** pile.

neck

Your **neck** is the part of your body that joins your head to your shoulders.

need (needing, needed)

If you **need** something, you must have it. All plants and animals **need** water to live.

needle

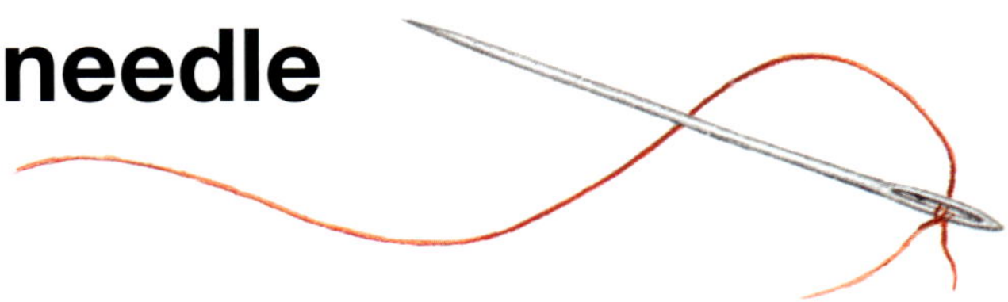

1 A **needle** is a long, thin, pointed piece of metal that you use for sewing. It has a hole at the top that thread goes through. Another kind of **needle** is used for knitting.
2 A **needle** is also a thin, sharp, green leaf. Some kinds of trees, like pines, have **needles**.

neighbour

A **neighbour** is somebody who lives near you. Our **neighbours** are very friendly.

Some words, such as **knee**, sound as if they begin with **n**, but you will find them in the dictionary under **kn**.

nephew

Somebody's **nephew** is the son of their brother or sister.

nest

A **nest** is a home that an animal makes for its young. Birds build **nests** out of things like grass, mud and sticks.

net

A **net** is pieces of string tied together so that there are holes in between. People use **nets** to catch fish. **Nets** are also used in games like tennis and football.

never

Never means not at any time. I have **never** seen a giraffe.

new

1 Something that is **new** has never been used before. My mum bought me some **new** trainers yesterday.
2 **New** also means different. We have a **new** swimming teacher this term.

news

News is information about things that have just happened. Have you heard the **news**? Katie has got a new baby brother.

newspaper

A **newspaper** is sheets of paper printed with words and pictures about things that are going on in the world.

next

Next means the one that comes after this one. **Next** Saturday we are going to the beach.

nice

If something or somebody is **nice**, they make you feel good or you like them. This apple tastes **nice**.

niece

Somebody's **niece** is the daughter of their brother or sister.

night

Another word that sounds like **night** is **knight**.

Night is the part of the day when the sky is dark and the Sun does not shine. People sleep at **night**.

Some words, such as **knife**, sound as if they begin with **n**, but you will find them in the dictionary under **kn**.

nightmare

A **nightmare** is a frightening dream.

nod (nodding, nodded)

When you **nod**, you move your head up and down quickly as a way of saying "yes".

noise

A **noise** is a sound that somebody or something makes. I heard a strange **noise** outside my window.

noisy (noisier, noisiest)

Somebody or something that is **noisy** makes a lot of noise. Don't be so **noisy** – you will wake the baby up!

noon

Noon is 12 o'clock in the middle of the day.

normal

Normal means usual or ordinary. Will you be home at the **normal** time today?

north

North is a direction. If you look towards the Sun as it comes up in the morning, **north** is on your left.

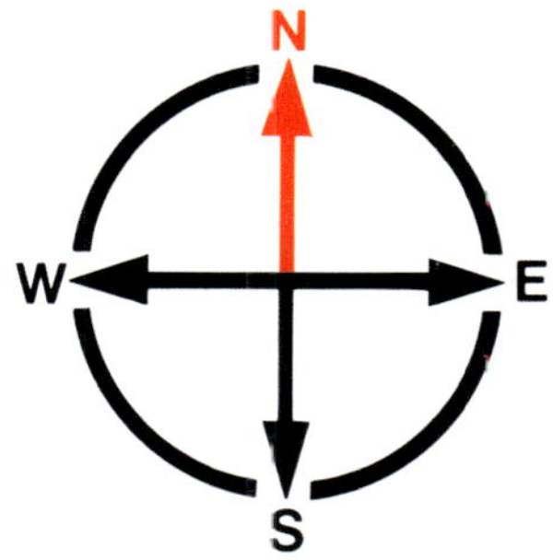

nose

Your **nose** is the part of your face you use for breathing and smelling.

Another word that sounds like **nose** is **knows**.

note

1 A **note** is a short letter to somebody. Sarah left me a **note** saying she had gone swimming.

2 A **note** is also a sound in music that you can play or sing.

notice

1 (noticing, noticed) If you **notice** something, you see it and think about it. Nadia **noticed** that Jamie was wearing a new coat.
2 A **notice** is a piece of paper or a sign with writing on it which tells people something. The **notice** said: "No dogs allowed".

now

Now means at this moment. You are reading this book **now**.

number

We use **numbers** when we count. 1, 2 and 3 are **numbers**. You can also write **numbers** as words (one, two, three).

nurse

A **nurse** is a person whose job is to look after people who are ill or hurt.

nut

A **nut** is a hard fruit that grows inside a very hard shell. Peanuts and hazelnuts are different kinds of **nuts**.

Word play
Trace this puzzle, then write in the answers using the pictures as clues.

Across 1

3 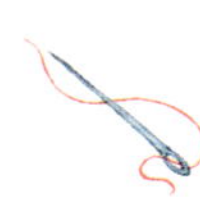 4

Down

1 

2 

3 

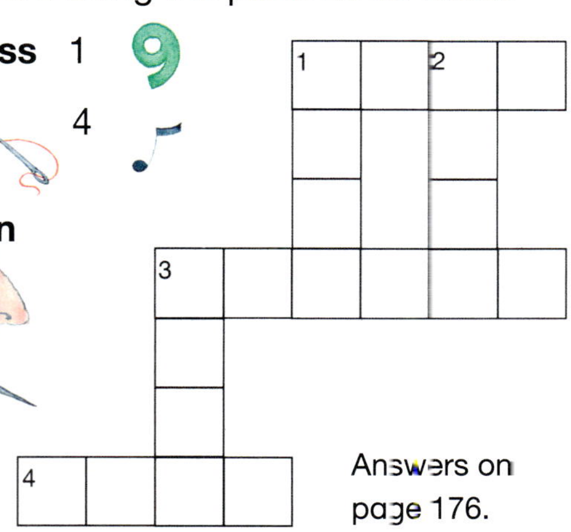

Answers on page 176.

oar

An **oar** is a long piece of wood with one flat end that you use for moving a boat through water.

> Another word that sounds like **oar** is **or**.

obey (obeying, obeyed)

When you **obey** somebody, you do what that person tells you to do. When I tell my dog to sit, he always **obeys** me.

ocean

An **ocean** is a very big sea. The Pacific and the Atlantic are **oceans**.

o'clock

O'clock is a word that you use to say what time it is. I get up at eight **o'clock** in the morning.

octopus

(octopuses)

An **octopus** is an animal that lives in the sea. It has eight long arms, called tentacles.

odd

1 An **odd** number is any number that ends in 1, 3, 5, 7 or 9. You cannot divide these numbers by 2 without leaving something over. The opposite of **odd** is even.

2 (odder, oddest)
If something is **odd**, it is strange. My bike is making an **odd** noise – I think it needs oil.

3 Odd things do not belong together in a pair or in a set. Rochelle is wearing **odd** socks!

office

An **office** is a place where people go to work. **Offices** have things like desks, chairs and computers.

often

If you do something **often**, you do it many times. We **often** go shopping on Saturday mornings.

oil

1 Oil is a smooth, thick liquid that comes from the ground. You can burn **oil** to make heat or to make machines move.
2 Oil is also a smooth liquid that people use for cooking. It comes from plants or animals.

old

1 Somebody who is **old** has lived for a long time. My grandfather is very **old** – he is ninety!
2 Something that is **old** was made a long time ago. Our house is very **old**. It was built two hundred years ago.
3 You also use **old** to talk about something that you had before. My **old** school was farther from home than my new one.

onion

An **onion** is a round vegetable with a strong taste and smell.

only

Only means no more than. There is **only** one chocolate left in the box.

open

1 If something like a door or a gate is **open**, you can go through it.
2 If something like a box is **open**, it is not closed or covered, so that you can see inside.

opposite

1 Opposite means different in every way. Good is the **opposite** of bad, and hot is the **opposite** of cold. (Look at the next page.)
2 Opposite also means on the other side. Paulo is sitting **opposite** Jenna.

orange

An **orange** is a round, sweet fruit with a thick skin.

orchestra

An **orchestra** is a large group of people playing different musical instruments together.

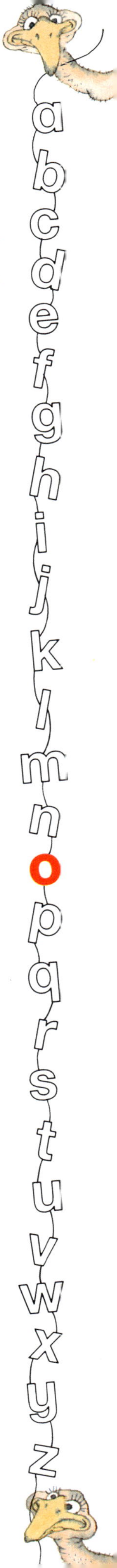

Opposites

light / heavy

high / low

closed / open

clean / dirty

happy / sad

little / big

old / young

long / short

hard / soft

Here are some more opposites. If you need to check their meanings, you can find them all in this dictionary.

rough / smooth	**hot / cold**
cheap / expensive	**tall / short**
deep / shallow	**loud / quiet**
tight / loose	**empty / full**
wide / narrow	**light / dark**

order

1 Order means the way that things follow one another. The letters of the alphabet always come in the same **order**.
2 (ordering, ordered) If you **order** something, you say you would like it. In the restaurant we **ordered** hamburgers and drinks.
3 If you **order** somebody to do something, you say that they must do it. The doctor **ordered** Michael to stay in bed.

ordinary

Something that is **ordinary** is not exciting or special in any way. Yesterday was my birthday, but today is just an **ordinary** day.

ostrich (ostriches)

An **ostrich** is a large bird with long legs and a long neck. **Ostriches** cannot fly.

otter

An **otter** is a small animal with brown fur. **Otters** can swim very well and they catch fish to eat.

oval

Something that is **oval** is shaped like an egg.

oven

An **oven** is the part inside a cooker where you put food to cook it.

over

Over means above. I threw the ball **over** my friend's head.

owe (owing, owed)

If you **owe** somebody something, you must give it to them. Jamie lent me 70p for an ice cream yesterday, so I **owe** him 70p.

owl

An **owl** is a bird that hunts small animals at night.

Owls have large, round eyes and they can see well in the dark.

own (owning, owned)

If you **own** something, it belongs to you. Do you know who **owns** that car?

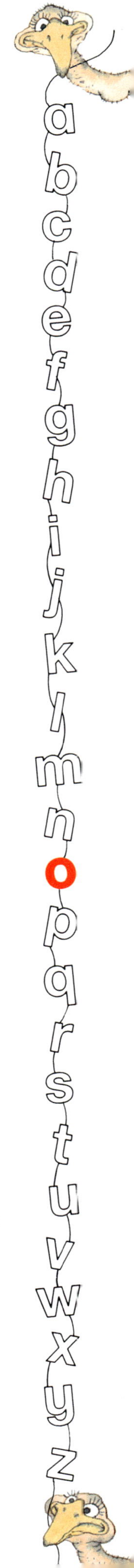

pack (packing, packed)

When you **pack** a bag or a box, you put clothes and other things inside it.

package

A **package** is something in a box or envelope that you send in the post.

paddle

A **paddle** is a short oar that you use for moving a canoe through water.

page

A **page** is one side of a piece of paper in a book. This book has a lot of **pages**.

paid Look at **pay**.

pain

A **pain** is the feeling that you have in a part of your body when it hurts. I have got a **pain** in my stomach.

paint

1 Paint is a liquid that we use to make pictures or to put colour on something.
2 (painting, painted) When you **paint** a picture, you make a picture using paints. Gemma is **painting** a rainbow.
3 (painting, painted) When you **paint** something like a wall, you put paint on it. I helped mum **paint** the door red.

painting

A **painting** is a picture that somebody has painted. The teacher put our **paintings** up on the wall.

pair

1 A **pair** is two things that you use together, like shoes. I have a new **pair** of gloves.
2 You also use **pair** to talk about things like scissors and trousers which have two parts the same joined together.

Another word that sounds like **pair** is **pear**.

palace

A **palace** is a very large house with a lot of rooms. People like kings, queens and presidents live in **palaces**.

pale

Something that is **pale** is almost white. You look very **pale** – are you feeling ill?

palm

Your **palm** is the flat inside part of your hand, between your fingers and your wrist.

pan

A **pan** is a metal container with a handle. You use it for cooking food in.

pancake

A **pancake** is a thin, round cake made from flour, eggs and milk and cooked in a pan in hot oil.

panda

A **panda** is a black and white animal that looks like a bear. **Pandas** come from China.

pant (panting, panted)

When you **pant**, you breathe quickly. The dog was **panting** because she had run up the stairs.

paper

Paper is a something that people use for writing on or for wrapping things in. The pages of books are also made of **paper**.

parachute

A **parachute** is a thing like a big umbrella made of light, strong cloth. It lets people float slowly down through the air when they jump out of an aeroplane.

parcel

A **parcel** is something wrapped in paper that can be sent in the post. My auntie sent me a **parcel** on my birthday.

parent

A **parent** is a mother or a father.

park

1 A **park** is a place with grass and trees where anybody can go to walk or play games. We had a picnic in the **park**.

2 (parking, parked) When somebody **parks** a car, they stop and leave it somewhere for a short time. Ian **parked** outside the school.

a b c d e f g h i j k l m n o p q r s t u v w x y z

parrot

A **parrot** is a bird with brightly coloured feathers. Many people keep **parrots** as pets. Some **parrots** can learn to talk.

part

A **part** is a piece of something. Your hands and your head are **parts** of your body.

party (parties)

A **party** is a group of people having fun together. We went to Rosie's birthday **party** on Saturday.

pass (passes, passing, passed)

1 If you **pass** somebody or something, you go by them. Do you **pass** any shops on your way to school?
2 When you **pass** something to somebody, you give it to them. Please could you **pass** me the scissors?

passenger

A **passenger** is a person who is travelling in a car, bus, train, ship or an aeroplane.

past

1 The **past** is the time before now. In the **past**, people did not have cars.
2 **Past** means after. It's twelve minutes **past** six.

paste

Paste is soft, wet stuff that you use for sticking paper and other things together.

pastry

Pastry is flour, fat and water mixed together and rolled until it is flat, then baked. **Pastry** is used for making pies.

path

A **path** is a narrow piece of land for people to walk along. There is a **path** across the fields.

patient

1 A **patient** is a person who is ill and who is being looked after by a doctor or a nurse.
2 If you are **patient**, you can wait for something to happen without getting cross. Just be **patient** – it will soon be your turn.

pattern

A **pattern** is how lines, colours and shapes look on something. These pieces of paper have different **patterns** on them.

paw

A **paw** is an animal's foot. A cat has four **paws**.

pay (pays, paying, paid)

When you **pay** somebody, you give them money for something. My dad **paid** the driver for taking us home.

pea

A **pea** is a small, round, green vegetable. **Peas** grow in long, green things called pods.

peace

Peace is a time when it is quiet, without any wars or fighting.

Another word that sounds like **peace** is **piece**.

peach (peaches)

A **peach** is a soft, round fruit with a yellow and red skin and a stone in the middle.

peacock

A **peacock** is a large, male bird with beautiful, long blue and green feathers in its tail. The female is called a **peahen**.

peanut

A **peanut** is a nut with a brown shell. **Peanuts** grow under the ground.

pear

A **pear** is a fruit that is green or yellow on the outside and white on the inside.

Another word that sounds like **pear** is **pair**.

pebble

A **pebble** is a small, round, smooth stone. You often see **pebbles** on beaches.

pedal

A **pedal** is a part of a machine that you press with your feet to make it move or work. A bike has **pedals**.

peel

1 Peel is the skin on some fruits and vegetables. Potatoes, apples and oranges all have **peel**.
2 (peeling, peeled) If you **peel** something, you take the skin off it. Rosa and Thomas are **peeling** some fruit.

pen

A **pen** is a long, thin tool filled with ink that you use for writing with.

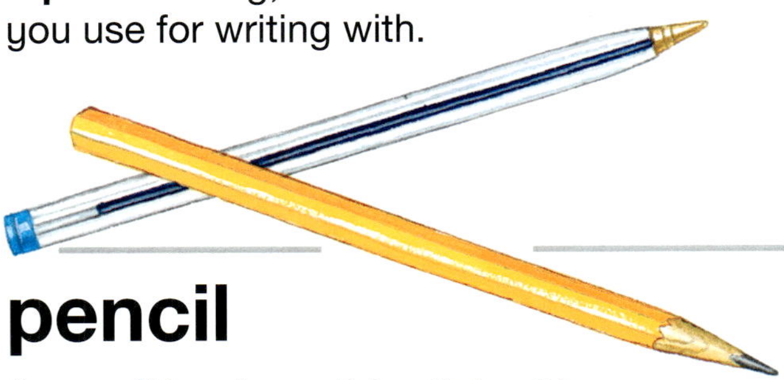

pencil

A **pencil** is a long, thin stick with grey or coloured stuff in the middle. You use it for writing or drawing with.

penguin

A **penguin** is a large black and white bird that lives in very cold parts of the world. **Penguins** can swim well, but they cannot fly.

people

Men, women and children are **people**.

pepper

1 Pepper is a powder with a hot taste that you can put on food.
2 A **pepper** is a bright red, green or yellow vegetable. I'd like **peppers** on my pizza.

perch (perches, perching, perched)

To **perch** means to sit on the edge of something. Birds often **perch** on branches.

perfume

Perfume is a liquid with a nice smell.

person

A **person** is a man, a woman or a child.

pet

A **pet** is an animal like a dog, a hamster or a parrot that you keep and look after in your home. Do you have any **pets**?

petal

Petals are the soft, thin, coloured parts of a flower.

phone

Phone is short for **telephone**.

photograph

A **photograph** is a picture that you take with a camera. The short word for **photograph** is **photo**.

piano (pianos)

A **piano** is a large musical instrument. It has black and white keys that you press to make sounds. My brother is learning to play the **piano**.

pick (picking, picked)

1 When you **pick** something, you take it because it is the one that you want. **Pick** the colour that you like best.
2 If you **pick** flowers or fruit, you take them from the place where they are growing. We **picked** apples from the tree in the garden.
3 When you **pick** something up, you lift it. I bent down to **pick** up my pencil from the floor.

picnic

A **picnic** is a meal that you take with you and eat outside. We had a **picnic** by the river.

picture

A **picture** is a drawing, a painting or a photograph.

pie

A **pie** is meat or fruit covered with pastry and cooked in an oven. I like apple **pie** with cream.

piece

A **piece** is a part of something. Would you like a **piece** of cake?

Another word that sounds like **piece** is **peace**.

pig

A **pig** is an animal that is kept on farms. **Pigs** are quite fat and they have short legs, flat noses and curly tails. A young **pig** is called a piglet.

pigeon

A **pigeon** is a fat grey or brown bird. You can often see **pigeons** in towns.

pile

A **pile** is a lot of things on top of one another.

Sapphire has a big **pile** of books.

pill

A **pill** is a small, round piece of medicine that you swallow. The doctor gave my mum some **pills** when she was ill.

pillow

A **pillow** is a soft cushion that you put your head on when you are in bed.

pilot

A **pilot** is a person who flies an aeroplane.

pin

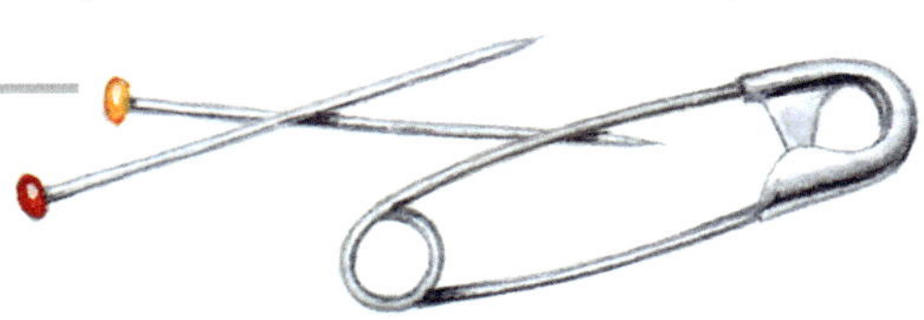

A **pin** is a small, thin piece of metal with a sharp point at one end. **Pins** are used for holding pieces of cloth or paper together.

pipe

A **pipe** is a long tube that carries things like water, oil or gas from one place to another.

pirate

A **pirate** is a person who robs ships at sea.

pizza

A **pizza** is a flat, round food that is baked in an oven. It is made of a kind of bread with things like tomatoes and cheese on top.

place

A **place** is an area or a building where something is. We took photos of all the **places** we visited on holiday.

plain

Something that is **plain** is all one colour and has no pattern on it. Lily is wearing a **plain** blue dress.

Another word that sounds like **plain** is **plane**.

plan (planning, planned)

When you **plan** something, you decide what you are going to do and how to do it. We are **planning** what to do in the summer holidays.

plane

A **plane** is a machine that flies. **Planes** have wings and engines. **Plane** is short for **aeroplane**.

> Another word that sounds like **plane** is **plain**.

planet

A **planet** is a big, round thing in space that moves around a star. Earth is one of the nine **planets** travelling around the Sun. (Look at the next page.)

plant

A **plant** is anything that grows in earth. Trees and flowers are **plants**.

plaster

1 A **plaster** is a piece of sticky material that you use to cover a cut on your body.
2 **Plaster** is soft stuff that goes hard when it dries. **Plaster** is used to cover walls and ceilings inside buildings.

plastic

Plastic is a strong, light material that is made in factories. **Plastic** is used to make a lot of different things, like bags and buckets.

plate

A **plate** is a round, flat thing that you put food on.

play

1 (playing, played) When you **play**, you do something to enjoy yourself. We are **playing** in the garden. Do you want to **play** a game with us?
2 (playing, played) When you **play** a musical instrument, you make sounds with it. I'm learning to **play** the guitar.
3 (plays) A **play** is a story that you watch on television or in the theatre, or listen to on the radio.

playground

A **playground** is a place outside where children can play.

Word play
Mend the broken plates and make some words for things to eat.

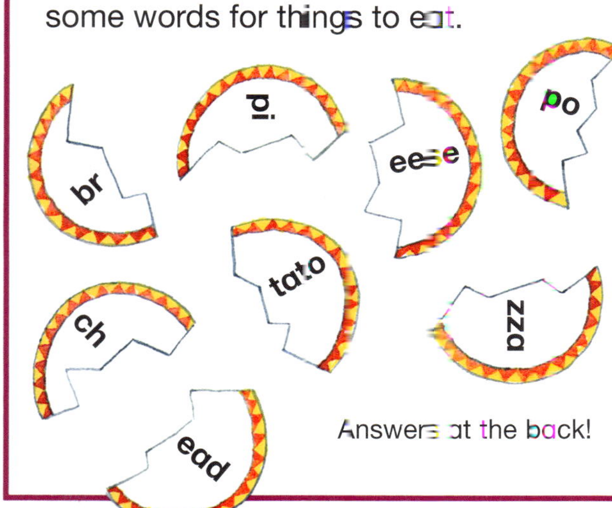

Answers at the back!

Planets

Light and dark
It gets dark at night because the Earth spins as it travels round the Sun. You can see how this works by slowly turning a globe while a light is shining on it.

please

You say **please** when you are asking somebody to do something. **Please** can you close the door?

plenty

If there is **plenty** of something, there is more than you need. Why don't you stay for dinner? There is **plenty** of food.

plus

You use **plus** to talk about adding numbers together. Four **plus** two is six.

pocket

A **pocket** is a small bag that is sewn into clothes. **Pockets** are for putting things in.

poem

A **poem** is a piece of writing. **Poems** usually have short lines, and the last words of the lines sometimes rhyme.

point

1 A **point** is the sharp end of something, like a pin or a pencil.
2 You win a **point** in a game or sport when you do well. In the quiz, our team got ten **points**.
3 (pointing, pointed)
If you **point**, you show where something is by using your finger.

pointed

Something that is **pointed** has a sharp end. The witch is wearing a long, **pointed** hat.

poisonous

Something that is **poisonous** can kill you or make you ill if you eat it. Don't pick those berries because they are **poisonous**.

polar bear

A **polar bear** is a big, white bear that lives in a very cold part of the Earth.

pole

A **pole** is a long, thin piece of wood or metal. The tent is held in place by metal **poles**.

police

The **police** are people whose job is to make sure that everybody obeys the law.

polite

If you are **polite**, you behave well and you are not rude. It is **polite** to say "thank you" when somebody gives you something.

pond

A **pond** is a small lake. The **pond** in our garden has fish and frogs in it.

pony (ponies)

A **pony** is a kind of small horse.

pool

A **pool** is an area filled with water for swimming in.

poor

Somebody who is **poor** does not have a lot of money.

popcorn

Popcorn is a food made from a kind of corn that bursts open when you cook it.

possible

Something that is **possible** can be done. It is **possible** to fly faster than the speed of sound.

post

1 The **post** is the letters and parcels that are sent and delivered. A letter from my cousin came in the **post** today.
2 (posting, posted) If you **post** a letter or a parcel, you send it. Can you **post** this card for me, please?

post office

A **post office** is a building where you can buy stamps and send letters and parcels.

pot

A **pot** is a deep, round container. Dad made the soup in a big **pot**. We often grow plants in **pots**.

potato (potatoes)

A **potato** is a vegetable that grows under the ground. **Potatoes** are brown on the outside and white on the inside.

pour (pouring, poured)

When you **pour** a liquid, you make it run out of a container. Jenna is **pouring** some milk into the bowl.

powder

A **powder** is something that is made up of a lot of very small pieces. Flour is a **powder** and so is dust.

power

Power is the strength to make something happen. Cars get the **power** to move from petrol.

practise (practising, practised)

When you **practise** something, you do it lots of times so that you get better at it. If you want to play the guitar well, you need to **practise** every day.

prepare (preparing, prepared)

If you **prepare** something, you get it ready. I helped my dad to **prepare** dinner.

present

1 A **present** is something that you give to somebody.

I gave Paul a **present** for his birthday.

2 The **present** is now. I'm too busy to help you at **present**.

president

A **president** is a person that other people have chosen to lead a country.

press (presses, pressing, pressed)

When you **press** something, you push hard on it. You **press** these keys to play a tune.

pretend (pretending, pretended)

If you **pretend**, you try to make people believe something that is not true. Andrew is **pretending** to be asleep.

pretty (prettier, prettiest)

Somebody or something that is **pretty** is nice to look at. Flowers are **pretty**.

price

The **price** of something is how much money you have to pay for it.

The **price** of the lamp is written on the label.

prince

A **prince** is the son or the grandson of a king or a queen.

princess (princesses)

A **princess** is the daughter or the granddaughter of a king or a queen.

a b c d e f g h i j k l m n o **p** q r s t u v w x y z

print (printing, printed)

When somebody **prints** words and pictures, they put them on to paper using a machine. This book was **printed**.

prison

A **prison** is a building where people have to stay because they have done something that is against the law.

prize

A **prize** is something that people win for doing well. Lucy won first **prize** for her painting.

problem

A **problem** is something that is difficult to understand, decide or answer. If you have any **problems**, ask somebody to help you.

programme

A **programme** is something that you watch or listen to on television or radio. Did you see that **programme** about snakes on television last night?

project

A **project** is a piece of work that you do at school. You find out all about something and write about it. Our class is doing a **project** on pets.

promise (promising, promised)

When you **promise**, you say that you will do or not do something. If I tell you what I'm going to give Hassan for his birthday, will you **promise** not to tell him?

protect (protecting, protected)

To **protect** something means to keep it safe. Gemma is wearing goggles to **protect** her eyes when she goes swimming.

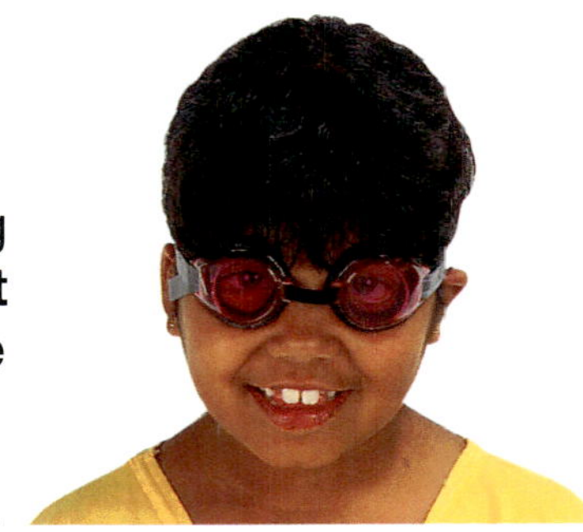

proud

If you are **proud**, you are pleased about something good that you have done or about something that is yours. Sam is very **proud** of his new bike.

prove (proving, proved or proven)

When you **prove** something, you show that it is true. Scientists have **proved** that the Earth is round.

pudding

A **pudding** is something sweet that you eat at the end of your dinner.

puddle

A **puddle** is a small amount of liquid on the ground. Don't step in that **puddle**!

pull (pulling, pulled)

When you **pull** something, you hold it and move it towards you.

puncture

A **puncture** is a hole in a tyre. My bike has got a **puncture**.

punish (punishes, punishing, punished)

To **punish** somebody means to make them hurt because they have done something wrong. Ben's mum **punished** him for telling lies by sending him to bed early.

pupil

A **pupil** is somebody who is learning something at school. There are twenty-five **pupils** in my class.

puppet

A **puppet** is a kind of doll that can be made to move. Some **puppets** have a space inside where you can put your hand. Others have strings that you pull.

puppy (puppies)

A **puppy** is a young dog. Our dog has just had three **puppies**.

pure

Something that is **pure** is not mixed with anything else. The King's crown was made of **pure** gold.

purse

A **purse** is a small bag that people keep their money in.

push (pushes, pushing, pushed)

When you **push** something, you move it away from you. Ella is **pushing** her new toy along.

puzzle

A **puzzle** is a game, a question or a toy that you have fun trying to work out.

pyjamas

Pyjamas are trousers and a jacket that you wear in bed.

quack (quacking, quacked)

When a duck **quacks**, it makes a loud noise.

quarter

A **quarter** is one of four equal parts of something. Four **quarters** make a whole.

queen

A **queen** is a woman who rules a country, or the wife of a king.

question

You ask a **question** when you want to find out about something. I asked my teacher a **question** about when dinosaurs lived.

queue

A **queue** is a line of people who are waiting for something. There was a long **queue** at the bus stop.

quick

1 If somebody or something is **quick**, they move fast. Be **quick** or we'll miss the start of the film.
2 Quick also means done in a short time. We only had time for a **quick** lunch because we were late.

quiet

When somebody or something is **quiet**, they make a small amount of noise or no noise at all. Be **quiet** or you will wake the baby up!

quite

1 Quite means more than a little bit. It's **quite** hot today.
2 Not **quite** means almost. Dinner is not **quite** ready.

quiz (quizzes)

A **quiz** is a kind of game. In a **quiz**, somebody asks a lot of questions to find out how much you know. Our team won the **quiz** because we got all the answers right.

rabbit

A **rabbit** is a small wild animal with long ears and soft fur. Some people keep **rabbits** as pets.

race

You have a **race** to find out who or what can go the fastest. Michael won the **race**.

radio (radios)

A **radio** is a machine that brings sounds through the air so that you can hear them. You turn on a **radio** to listen to music, news and other programmes.

raft

A **raft** is a kind of flat boat. **Rafts** are often made of lots of pieces of wood joined together.

railway (railways)

A **railway** is a kind of path made of metal bars for trains to run along.

rain

1 Rain is water that falls from the clouds in small drops.

2 (raining, rained) When it is **raining**, drops of water are falling from the sky.

rainbow

A **rainbow** is a curve of different colours that you sometimes see in the sky when the sun shines through rain.

raise (raising, raised)

When you **raise** something, you lift it up. If you know the answer to the question, please **raise** your hand.

rake

A **rake** is a tool that you use in the garden. Some **rakes** are used for collecting leaves and grass into piles and others are used for making the earth smooth.

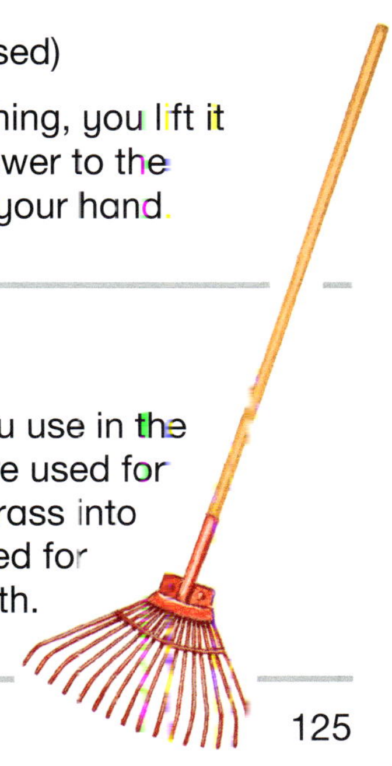

ran
Look at **run**.

rang
Look at **ring**.

rat

A **rat** is an animal that looks like a big mouse. **Rats** have long tails and sharp teeth.

rattle
(rattling, rattled)

To **rattle** means to make the sound of things knocking together. The coins **rattled** in the tin.

raw
Food that is **raw** has not been cooked. Salads are usually made of **raw** vegetables.

reach
(reaching, reached)

1 When you **reach** for something, you put your hand out towards it.

Eden is not tall enough to **reach** the ceiling.

2 When you **reach** a place, you arrive there. It was very late when we **reached** grandma's house.

read
*say *reed*
(reading, read *say *red*)

When you **read**, you look at words and understand what they mean.

Omer is **reading** an interesting book.

ready
If you are **ready**, you can do something straight away. We'll go out as soon as you are **ready**.

real
Something that is **real** is true or it is not a copy. This isn't a **real** spider. It's made of plastic.

really
Really means that something is true. Did the magician **really** make the rabbit disappear or was it just a trick?

reason
A **reason** explains why something happens or why you do something. The **reason** why we're late is that we missed the bus.

record
1 A **record** is a flat, round piece of plastic that plays music or other sounds when it turns on a **record-player**.
2 A **record** is also the best that has ever been done. What is the world **record** for the 100-metre race?

rectangle

A **rectangle** is a shape with four sides and four corners. This page is in the shape of a **rectangle**.

refrigerator

A **refrigerator** is a big metal box where you can put food to keep it cold and fresh. The short word for refrigerator is **fridge**.

refuse (refusing, refused)

If you **refuse**, you say you will not do something that somebody has asked you to do. Dad asked my sister to tidy her room but she **refused**.

reindeer
(reindeer)

A **reindeer** is a large deer that lives in cold countries.

remember (remembering, remembered)

If you **remember** something, you keep it in your mind or bring it back into your mind. Can you **remember** what you did on your birthday last year?

remind (reminding, reminded)

To **remind** means to make somebody remember something. Can you **remind** me to phone David tomorrow?

repeat (repeating, repeated)

If you **repeat** something, you do it or say it again. Could you **repeat** what you said? I didn't hear you the first time.

reply (replies, replying, replied)

When you **reply**, you give an answer. "Where have you been?" "Swimming," she **replied**.

snake

lizard

tortoise

reptile

A **reptile** is an animal that has cold blood and skin covered in scales. **Reptiles** lay eggs. Snakes, tortoises and lizards are **reptiles**.

rescue
(rescuing, rescued)

If you **rescue** somebody, you save them from danger. The helicopter **rescued** the man whose boat had sunk.

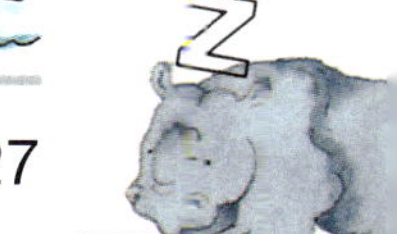

rest

1 When you have a **rest**, you stop what you are doing for a time because you are tired. Maria needed a **rest** after working hard in the garden all morning.
2 The **rest** is what is left after everything else has gone. I ate half of the orange and gave the **rest** to my friend.

restaurant

A **restaurant** is a place where people go to buy and eat meals. We went to a **restaurant** on my dad's birthday.

Word play
The box on the opposite page tells you that another word that sounds like **right** is **write**. Can you find another word that sounds like:

tail hole way dear plane

Look up these words in the dictionary if you need any help.

Answers at the back!

return (returning, returned)

1 When you **return**, you come back or go back. When do you **return** to school after the summer holidays?
2 When you **return** something, you give it back. I am going to **return** this book to the library when I have finished reading it.

rhinoceros (rhinoceroses)

Rhinoceros comes from two Greek words that mean 'nose horn'.

A **rhinoceros** is a big, heavy wild animal with a thick skin and one or two horns on its nose. **Rhinoceroses** live in Africa and Asia. They are called **rhinos** for short.

rhyme (rhyming, rhymed)

When words **rhyme**, they have the same sound at the end. Red **rhymes** with bed, and house **rhymes** with mouse.

ribbon

A **ribbon** is a long, thin piece of cloth or paper.

rice

Rice is a kind of food. It is the small, white seeds of a plant that get soft when they are cooked. **Rice** plants grow in wet ground in hot countries.

rich

Somebody who is **rich** has a lot of money. If I were **rich**, I would live in a big palace and I would go everywhere by plane.

ridden Look at **ride**.

riddle

A **riddle** is a strange question that has a funny or clever answer. The answer to the **riddle** "What goes up when the rain comes down?" is "an umbrella".

ride

1 (riding, rode, ridden) When you **ride** a horse or a bike, you sit on it as it moves along. I love **riding** my new bike.
2 When you have a **ride** in something like a car or a bus, you travel in it. The farmer gave me a **ride** in his tractor.

right

Another word that sounds like **right** is **write**.

1 Right is the opposite of left. Rosa has a glove puppet on her **right** hand.
2 If something is **right**, there are no mistakes. I got all my sums **right**.

ring

1 A **ring** is a small circle of metal that you wear around your finger.
2 A **ring** is also a circle with an empty centre. The children sat in a **ring** around the teacher.
3 (ringing, rang, rung) To **ring** is to make the sound of a bell. The telephone is **ringing** – will somebody please answer it?

ripe

When fruit is **ripe**, it is ready to eat. This banana is not **ripe** yet – it's still green.

rise (rising, rose, risen)

To **rise** means to move up. The Sun **rises** in the east every morning.

river

A **river** is a lot of moving water with land on both sides. A **river** flows into a lake or into the sea.

road

A **road** is a wide path leading from one place to another for cars, lorries, bicycles and buses to travel along.

> Another word that sounds like **road** is **rode**.

roar (roaring, roared)

To **roar** means to make a loud noise like a lion makes. We heard the plane's engines **roar** just before it took off.

rob (robbing, robbed)

To **rob** means to take something that does not belong to you. The men who **robbed** the bank stole thousands of pounds.

robber

A **robber** is somebody who steals things from somebody or from a place.

robin

A **robin** is a small bird with red feathers on the front of its body.

robot

A **robot** is a machine that can do some of the same work that people do. In factories, a lot of work is now done by **robots**.

rock

1 Rock is the very hard stuff that mountains are made of. Pieces of this are called **rocks**.
2 (rocking, rocked) If you **rock** something, you move it gently backwards and forwards or from side to side. Dad **rocked** the baby in his arms.

rocket

A **rocket** is a big machine for travelling into space. It is in the shape of a tube with burning gases inside that make it fly into the sky.

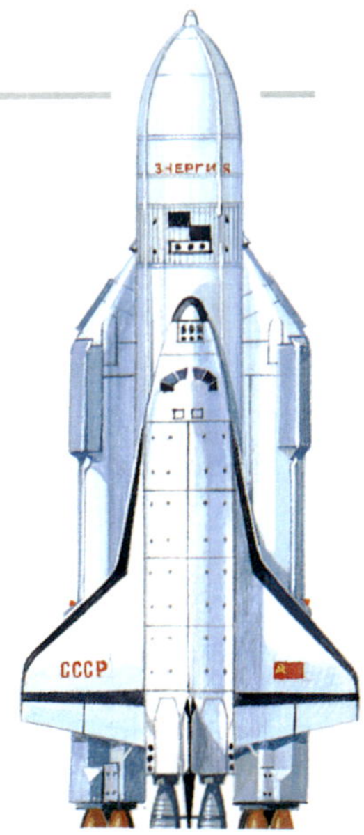

rode Look at **ride**.

> Another word that sounds like **rode** is **road**.

roll

1 (rolling, rolled) When something like a ball **rolls**, it moves along by turning over and over. Jenny **rolled** the ball down the hill.
2 A **roll** of something like cloth or tape is a long piece of it that has been wrapped around itself lots of times.
3 A **roll** is also a round piece of bread for one person to eat. I had a cheese and salad **roll** for lunch.

Some words, such as **wrong**, sound as if they begin with **r**, but you will find them in the dictionary under **wr**.

roof

A **roof** is the part on top that covers a building or something like a car or a bus.

room

1 A **room** is a part inside a building. Bathrooms, bedrooms and kitchens are **rooms**.
2 Room is also space. There is not enough **room** in our car for ten people!

root

The **roots** of a plant are the parts that grow under the ground. A plant takes in food and water through its **roots**.

rope

A **rope** is a very strong, thick string. People use **ropes** to lift and pull heavy things.

rose

1 A **rose** is a flower with lots of petals and sharp pointed parts called thorns on its stem. **Roses** usually smell nice.
2 Look at **rise**.

rough *say *ruff*

Something that is **rough** is not smooth. A cat's tongue feels **rough**.

round

1 Something that is **round** has the same shape as a circle or a ball.
2 Round also means on all sides of something. There is a wall **round** our garden.

row *rhymes with *go*

1 A **row** is a line of people or things. Our teacher asked us all to sit in a **row**.
2 (rowing, rowed) When you **row** a boat, you move it along by using oars. We **rowed** up the river.

rub (rubbing, rubbed)

When you **rub** something, you move your hand or another thing backwards and forwards across it.

Felicity is **rubbing** out her picture.

rubber

1 Rubber is a strong material that stretches and bounces and keeps out water. Tyres are made of black **rubber**.
2 A **rubber** is a small piece of rubber that we use to make pencil marks disappear.

rubbish

Rubbish is things that you throw away because you do not want them.

ruby (rubies)

A **ruby** is a red jewel that is worth a lot of money.

rug

A **rug** is a small piece of thick cloth that you use to cover part of a floor. There is a **rug** beside my bed.

ruin (ruining, ruined)

If something is **ruined**, it is spoilt. The rain **ruined** our picnic.

Word play
Match a picture clue on the left with one on the right to make four new words.

Answers at the back!

rule

1 A **rule** tells you that you must do something or that you must not do it. In football it is against the **rules** to touch the ball with your hand.
2 (ruling, ruled) To **rule** means to control a country and the people who live there. The King **ruled** his country well.

ruler

1 A **ruler** is a piece of wood, metal or plastic that you use for drawing or measuring straight lines.
2 A **ruler** is also a person who is the leader of a country.

rumble (rumbling, rumbled)

To **rumble** means to make a sound like thunder. The big lorry **rumbled** past.

run (running, ran, run)

When you **run**, you go somewhere by moving your legs quickly.

Robert had to **run** for the bus because he was late.

rung Look at **ring**.

rush (rushing, rushed)

If you **rush**, you go somewhere or do something quickly. We **rushed** home from school to play with our new puppy.

sad (sadder, saddest)

If you are **sad**, you feel unhappy. I felt **sad** when my best friend went away.

safe

If you are **safe**, you are not in any danger. The lost puppy was found **safe** and well.

said Look at **say**.

sail

A **sail** is a big piece of cloth on a boat. The wind blows against the **sail** and moves the boat along.

salad

A **salad** is a cold food made of different vegetables and other things mixed together.

salt

Salt is a white powder that people put on their food. Sea water has **salt** in it.

same

If two things are the **same**, they are just like each other.

Alice's socks are the **same** as José's.

sand

Sand is a kind of powder made of lots of very small pieces of rock. You can see **sand** by the sea and in deserts.

sandwich (sandwiches)

A **sandwich** is two slices of bread with food in between them. I had a **sandwich** for lunch.

sang Look at **sing**.

sank Look at **sink**.

sat Look at **sit**.

saucepan

A **saucepan** is a metal pot for cooking food. It has a lid and a long handle.

saucer

A **saucer** is a kind of small plate for putting a cup on.

save (saving, saved)

1 If you **save** somebody, you take them away from danger. The man jumped into the river and **saved** the child from drowning.

2 If you **save** money or something else, you keep it somewhere to use later. I'm **saving** up for a new computer game.

saw

1 Look at **see**.
2 A **saw** is a tool for cutting wood. It has a blade with sharp points like teeth along one edge.

say (saying, said)

When you **say** something, you make words with your mouth. Lucy **said** she was sorry.

scales

1 You use **scales** to find out how heavy somebody or something is.

Joe stood on the **scales** to weigh himself.

2 Scales are also the small, hard, flat things that cover the bodies of fish and reptiles.

scare (scaring, scared)

If something **scares** you, it makes you feel frightened. The monster in the film **scared** me when it suddenly appeared.

scarecrow

A **scarecrow** is a thing that looks like a person dressed in old clothes. Farmers put **scarecrows** in their fields to frighten off birds.

scarf (scarves)

A **scarf** is a long piece of cloth that you wear around your neck.

school

A **school** is a place where children go to learn. What did you do at **school** today?

science

Science is something that you can learn about at school. **Science** teaches us about things like animals and plants as well as about the Earth and other planets. A **scientist** is a person who finds out how things happen in **science**.

scissors

You use **scissors** for cutting. A pair of **scissors** has two sharp parts joined together.

score

1 In a game, the **score** is how many points each side has. At the end of the match the **score** was 4-2.
2 (scoring, scored) To **score** means to get a point in a game. In the quiz you **score** ten points if you get the right answer.

scratch
(scratches, scratching, scratched)

To **scratch** means to rub something sharp against something else. The cat is **scratching** the tree with its sharp claws.

scream (screaming, screamed)

If you **scream**, you call or shout in a loud voice. People **scream** when they are excited or frightened.

screen

A **screen** is a flat surface on which a film or a television programme is shown. Computers also have **screens**.

Another word that sounds like **sea** is **see**.

sea

A **sea** is a large area of salt water. Fish live in the **sea**. I like swimming in the **sea**.

seal

A **seal** is an animal with short, grey fur that lives in the sea and on land. **Seals** eat fish.

search (searches, searching, searched)

When you **search** for something, you look very carefully for it.

a b c d e f g h i j k l m n o p q r s t u v w x y z

seaside

The **seaside** is the land by the sea. We like swimming and playing in the sand when we go to the **seaside** for our holidays.

season

The **seasons** are the four parts of the year. They are called spring, summer, autumn and winter.

seat

A **seat** is anything that you sit on. Buses and cars have **seats**. We sat in the front **seats** when we went to see the film.

second

1 A **second** is a very short time. There are 60 **seconds** in a minute.
2 Second means next after the first. Sam won the race and I was **second**.

secret

A **secret** is something that only a few people know about. I can't tell you what's in the parcel. It's a **secret**!

see (seeing, saw, seen)

When you **see** something, you notice it with your eyes. My dad can't **see** well without his glasses.

Another word that sounds like **see** is **sea**.

seed

A **seed** is a very small, hard part of a plant. **Seeds** are put in the ground, and new plants grow from them.

seem (seeming, seemed)

To **seem** means to look or feel like something. Tara is tall, so she **seems** older than she really is.

seen Look at **see**.

seesaw

A **seesaw** is a toy. It has a long, flat part that two people sit on, one at each end, to go up and down.

sell (selling, sold)

If somebody **sells** something to you, they give it to you and you pay money. The woman was **selling** all kinds of vegetables.

send (sending, sent)

When you **send** something somewhere, you make it go there. I am **sending** this letter to my friend.

Some words, such as **centre**, sound as if they begin with **s**, but you will find them in the dictionary under **c**.

sensible

If you are **sensible**, you are good at deciding the right thing to do and you do not do anything silly. It was **sensible** of you to tell your teacher where you were going.

sent

Look at **send**.

sentence

A **sentence** is a group of words. A **sentence** begins with a capital letter (like A, B or C) and ends with a full stop (.).

set

A **set** is a group of things that belong together. I've got a new train **set**.

sew

(sewing, sewed, sewn)

When you **sew**, you join pieces of cloth together or join something to cloth using a needle and cotton.

Can you **sew** this button back on my shirt, please?

Another word that sounds like **sew** is **so**.

sex

(sexes)

The **sexes** are the two groups that people and animals belong to. The two **sexes** are males and females.

shadow

A **shadow** is a dark shape that you see near somebody or something that is in front of the light.

shake

(shaking, shook, shaken)

When you **shake** something, you move it quickly up and down or backwards and forwards.

shallow

Water that is **shallow** is not very deep. I am learning to swim in the **shallow** end of the pool.

shape

The **shape** of something is what you see if you draw a line around the outside of it. Circles, squares and triangles are all different **shapes**. (Look at the next page.)

Shapes

square
triangle
rectangle
circle
semicircle
oval
hexagon
octagon
star
crescent
diamond
heart
cube
cone
sphere
cylinder

share (sharing, shared)

1 If you **share** something, you give a part of it to somebody else. Alice is **sharing** her orange with her friends.
2 To **share** also means to use something together with another person. I **share** a bedroom with my sister.

shark

A **shark** is a very big fish with a lot of sharp teeth. **Sharks** live in the sea.

sharp

Something that is **sharp** has an edge or point that is good at cutting. Knives and scissors are usually **sharp**.

sheep (sheep)

A **sheep** is an animal that farmers keep for their thick wool and for their meat. A young **sheep** is called a lamb.

sheet

1 A **sheet** is a large piece of cloth for putting on a bed.
2 A **sheet** is also a thin, flat piece of something. May I have a **sheet** of paper?

shelf (shelves)

A **shelf** is a long, flat piece of wood fixed to a wall, where you can put things.

shell

A **shell** is the hard outside part of something. Eggs, nuts and snails have **shells**. The **shells** that you find on the beach once had animals living in them.

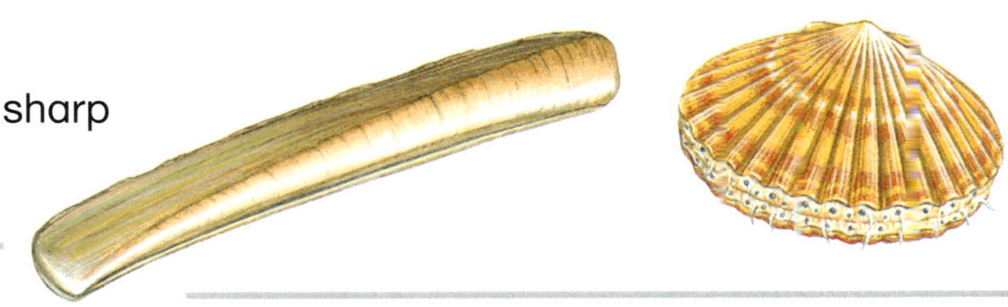

shelves Look at **shelf**.

shine (shining, shone)

When something **shines**, it gives out light, or it is bright like silver. The sun is **shining**. Something that is **shiny** is smooth and bright. Our new car is very **shiny**.

ship

A **ship** is a big boat for carrying people and things across the sea.

shirt

You wear a **shirt** on the top part of your body. A **shirt** has parts that cover your arms, and usually a collar and buttons.

shoe

You wear **shoes** on your feet. **Shoes** are usually made of leather or plastic. I am wearing blue **shoes** today.

shone Look at **shine**.

shook Look at **shake**.

shoot (shooting, shot)

1 To **shoot** means to make something go forwards from a thing like a bow or a gun. You **shoot** arrows from a bow.
2 To **shoot** also means to move somewhere very fast. Patrick **shot** out of the room.

shop

1 A **shop** is a place where you go to buy things.
2 (shopping, shopped) To **shop** means to buy things. We went **shopping** for food in the supermarket.

shore

The **shore** is the land along the edge of the sea or of a lake.

short

1 Something that is **short** is not very long. My brother has **short** hair. I wrote my grandma a **short** letter.
2 Somebody who is **short** is not very tall.

shot Look at **shoot**.

shoulder

Your **shoulder** is the top part of your arm where it joins your neck.

shout

(shouting, shouted)

When you **shout**, you say something very loudly.

Mia had to **shout** so that we could hear her.

show (showing, showed, shown)

1 When you **show** something, you let people see it. **Show** me your photos.
2 When you **show** somebody how to do something, you teach them how to do it. I **showed** my brother how to tie a bow.

shower

1 A **shower** is a place where you can wash by standing under water that is coming down on you.
2 A **shower** is also rain that falls for only a short time.

shown
Look at **show**.

shrink
(shrinking, shrank, shrunk)

When something **shrinks**, it gets smaller. These jeans **shrank** when they were washed.

shut
(shutting, shut)

When you **shut** a door, window, book or another thing, you move it so that it is not open. Please **shut** the window.

sick

When you are **sick**, you do not feel well.

side

1 The **side** of something is the left or right of it. You can see the alphabet at the **side** of this page.
2 The **sides** of something can also be its flat surfaces. This box has six **sides**.
3 The **sides** of something can also be the edges. A square has four **sides**.
4 The **sides** in a game are the teams that are playing against each other.

sign

1 A **sign** is a notice or a picture that tells you something.
2 (signing, signed) When you **sign** your name, you write it. **Sign** your name here.

silence

Silence means that there are no sounds. We waited in **silence** for the story to begin.

silly
(sillier, silliest)

If you say that somebody is being **silly**, you mean that they are not thinking carefully about what they are doing. It was very **silly** of you to run across the road without looking.

silver

Silver is a grey, shiny metal. Rings and necklaces are often made of **silver**.

sing
(singing, sang, sung)

When you **sing**, you make music with your voice. **Sing** that song again.

sink

1 (sinking, sank, sunk) When something **sinks**, it goes down under water. If you throw a stone into water, it will **sink**.
2 A **sink** is something in the kitchen where you can wash the dishes.

sister

Your **sister** is a girl who has the same mother and father as you.

Some words, such as **city**, sound as if they begin with **s**, but you will find them in the dictionary under **c**.

sit (sitting, sat)

When you **sit** somewhere, you rest your bottom there. Amy told her dog to **sit**.

size

The **size** of something is how big it is. What **size** shoes do you take? I take a **size** 10.

skate

1 Skates are special boots with wheels on the bottom that you wear for moving about on smooth ground.
2 Skates are also boots with sharp blades on the bottom that you wear for moving about on ice.

ski

Skis are long, flat, narrow pieces of metal, plastic or wood. You wear them with special boots to go fast on snow.

skin

Skin is what covers the outside of people, most animals and many plants. When you peel an orange, you take off its **skin**.

skip

(skipping, skipped)

When you **skip**, you move with little jumps from one foot to the other.

Mia is **skipping** with a rope.

skirt

A **skirt** is something that girls and women wear. It hangs down from the waist. Sara is wearing a blue **skirt**.

skull

Your **skull** is the round bone of your head. Your brain is inside your **skull**.

sky

The **sky** is the space above the Earth. You can often see the Moon and the stars in the **sky** at night.

sledge

A **sledge** is something that you sit on to ride on the snow. It has two long pieces of metal on the bottom which help it to slide along.

sleep (sleeping, slept)

When you **sleep**, you close your eyes and rest your whole body. People usually **sleep** at night.

slice

A **slice** is a thin, flat piece that has been cut from something. Can I have a **slice** of bread and butter, please?

slide

1 (sliding, slid) When something **slides**, it moves easily over another thing. The snake **slid** along the ground.
2 A **slide** is something that you play on. You climb up the steps on one side and then slide down the other side.

slip (slipping, slipped)

If you **slip**, you slide by mistake and fall down. I **slipped** on the wet floor.

slow

Somebody or something that is **slow** does not move quickly. Snails and tortoises are very **slow** animals.

small

Somebody or something that is **small** is not very big. This jumper is too **small** for me.

smash (smashes, smashed)

If something **smashes**, it breaks into a lot of pieces. I dropped the plate and it **smashed** on the floor.

smell (smelling, smelt or smelled)

1 When you **smell** something, you use your nose to find out about it. Jenna is **smelling** a rose.

2 When something **smells**, you find out about it using your nose. This soap **smells** lovely.

smile
(smiling, smiled)

When you **smile**, the corners of your mouth turn up to show that you are happy.

smoke

Smoke is the grey or black gas that goes up into the air when something is burning.

smooth

If something is **smooth**, you cannot feel any rough parts on it when you touch it. The glass in a window is **smooth**.

snail

A **snail** is a small creature with a hard shell on its back. **Snails** move along very slowly.

snake

A **snake** is a long, thin animal with no legs. It moves by sliding along the ground. **Snakes** are reptiles.

snap (snapping, snapped)

When something **snaps**, it makes a sudden, sharp sound. The pencil **snapped** when I stepped on it.

sneeze (sneezing, sneezed)

When you **sneeze**, you blow air out of your nose and mouth with a sudden, loud noise. You often **sneeze** when you have a cold.

snow

Snow is small, white pieces of frozen water that fall from the sky when the weather is very cold. Each piece of **snow** is called a **snowflake**. We like playing in the **snow**, making **snowballs** and building a **snowman**.

soap

People use **soap** with water for washing themselves. This bar of **soap** smells nice.

sock

Socks are soft things that you wear inside your shoes to cover your feet and the bottom parts of your legs.

sofa

A **sofa** is a soft seat with arms and a back. Two or three people can sit on a **sofa**.

soft

Something that is **soft** is not hard or firm. Kittens have **soft** fur.

soil

Soil is the brown stuff that plants grow in.

sold

Look at **sell**.

soldier

A **soldier** is somebody who is in an army. **Soldiers** fight in wars.

son

Somebody's **son** is a boy or a man who is their child.

Another word that sounds like **son** is **Sun**.

song

A **song** is a piece of music with words that you sing.

sore

If a part of your body feels **sore**, it hurts. My throat is **sore**.

sorry

If you are **sorry**, you are sad about something. I'm **sorry** I broke your pen.

sort

A **sort** is a kind. What **sort** of books do you like reading? I like adventure stories.

sound

A **sound** is something that you can hear. I heard the **sound** of a baby crying.

soup

Soup is a hot liquid food made from things like vegetables or meat. You eat **soup** with a spoon.

sour

Something that is **sour** has a taste that is not sweet. Lemons, and apples that are not ripe are **sour**.

south

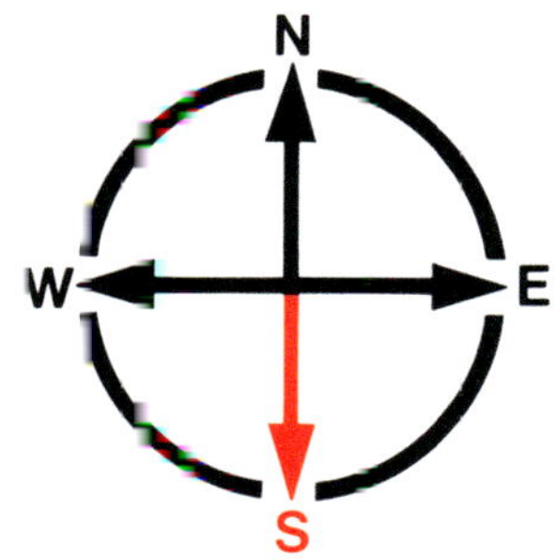

South is the direction that is on your right if you watch the Sun coming up in the morning.

space

1 Space is a place that has nothing in it. There is **space** here for you to put your box of toys.

2 Space is also the sky around the Earth and farther away, where all the stars and planets are.

spade

A **spade** is a tool with a long handle and a wide, flat part at the end. You use a **spade** for digging.

speak (speaking, spoke, spoken)

When you **speak**, you say words. I am **speaking** to my friend on the telephone.

special

1 If something is **special**, it is better or more important than other things. Today is a **special** day because it's my birthday.
2 Special also means made to do a job. You need a **special** camera for taking photos under water.

spell

1 (spelling, spelt or spelled) When you **spell** a word, you say or write the letters in the right order. "How do you **spell** 'spider'?" "S-p-i-d-e-r."
2 A **spell** is a magic trick that you can read about in stories. The fairy put a **spell** on the prince and turned him into a frog.

spend (spending, spent)

1 When you **spend** money, you pay for something. I have **spent** all my money on a present for my brother.
2 When you **spend** time, you use that time to do something. We **spent** our holiday at the beach.

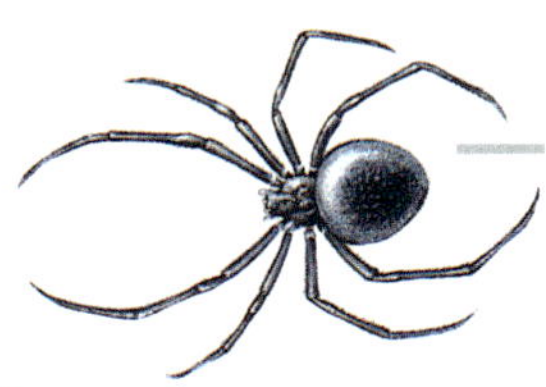

spider

A **spider** is a small creature with eight legs and no wings. **Spiders** spin webs to catch insects.

Spider comes from an old English word that meant 'spinner'

Word play
Look at the pictures and spell the words. The first letter of each word is given to help you. Use the dictionary to check your answers if you need to.

b

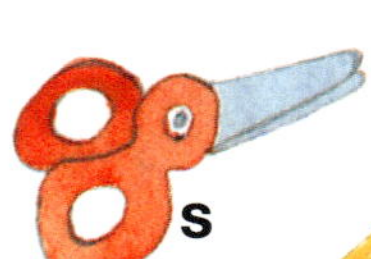
s

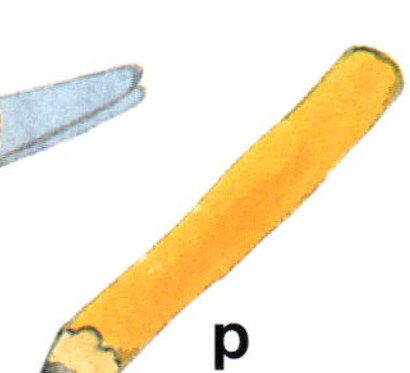
p

g

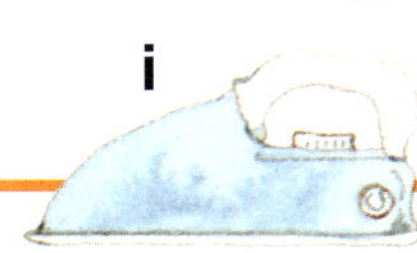
i

Answers at the back!

spill (spilling, spilt or spilled)

If you **spill** something, you make it flow out by mistake.

I **spilt** my drink all over the floor.

spin (spinning, spun)

1 When something **spins**, it turns round and round very fast. The Earth **spins** as it travels round the Sun.
2 Spin also means to pull cotton, wool or something else into a long, thin piece and twist it to make thread.

splash (splashing, splashed)

To **splash** means to make somebody or something wet with drops of liquid. My friend rode through a puddle on her bike and **splashed** us with dirty water.

spoil (spoiling, spoilt or spoiled)

If somebody **spoils** something, they make it less good than it was before. I **spoilt** my new shirt when I spilt paint on it.

spoke Look at **speak**.

spoken Look at **speak**.

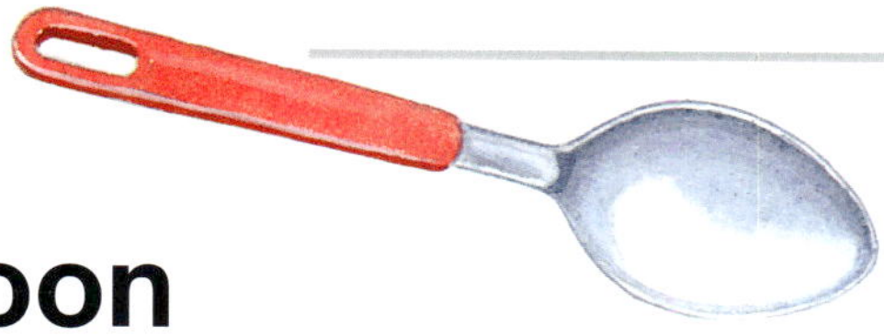

spoon

A **spoon** is a metal tool that you use for eating things like soup and cereals.

sport

A **sport** is a game or something else that you do to keep your body strong and well and to have fun. Football, tennis and running are all **sports**.

spot

1 A **spot** is a small, round mark. Leopards have yellow fur with dark **spots**.
2 A **spot** is also a small, red mark on your skin.

spring

1 Spring is the part of the year between winter and summer. In the **spring**, plants start to grow again.
2 A **spring** is a curly piece of metal that will jump back into the same shape if you press or pull it and then let it go.
3 (springing, sprang, sprung) To **spring** means to jump. The cat **sprang** up on to the wall.

spun

Look at **spin**.

square

A **square** is a shape with four straight sides that are the same length.

squash

(squashing, squashed)

If you **squash** something, you press it hard and make it flat.

squeeze

(squeezing, squeezed)

If you **squeeze** something, you press hard on the sides. You **squeeze** a toothpaste tube to make the toothpaste come out.

squirrel

A **squirrel** is a small animal with a big, thick tail. **Squirrels** live in trees.

stairs

Stairs are steps for going up or down inside a building.

Another word that sounds like **stairs** is **stares**.

stamp

A **stamp** is a small piece of paper with a picture and a price on it. You have to stick a **stamp** on a letter before you send it.

stand (standing, stood)

When you **stand** somewhere, you are on your feet. I am **standing** up because there is nowhere to sit.

star

1 A **star** is a very small, bright light that you see in the sky at night.
2 A **star** is also a shape with five or six points.

stare (staring, stared)

When you **stare**, you look hard at something for a long time. Everybody **stared** at the strange flying machine.

Another word that sounds like **stares** is **stairs**.

start (starting, started)

When you **start**, you do the first part of something. I am just **starting** to read my new book.

station

A **station** is a place where trains stop so that people can get on and off. We got off the train at Victoria **station**.

statue

A **statue** is the shape of a person or an animal, made of stone or metal.

stay (staying, stayed)

When you **stay** somewhere, you are there and you do not go away. My sister got up early, but I **stayed** in bed until ten o'clock.

steady (steadier, steadiest)

Something that is **steady** is not moving or shaking. Hold the ladder **steady** while I climb up.

steal (stealing, stole, stolen)

To **steal** means to take something that does not belong to you.

steam

Steam is a cloud of tiny drops of water that you see when water gets very hot.

stem

The **stem** of a plant is the long, thin part that grows above the ground.

step

1 A **step** is what you do when you lift your foot and put it down in a different place.

2 Steps are also the flat part of stairs where you put your foot to go up or down.

stick

1 A **stick** is a long, thin piece of wood.
2 (sticking, stuck) When you **stick** something, you fix it somewhere with glue or tape.
3 (sticking, stuck) When you **stick** a pointed thing like a pin into something else, you push it in. If you **stick** a pin into a balloon, it will burst.

still

1 If somebody or something is **still**, it is not moving. Please stand **still** while I take your photograph.
2 **Still** also means that something has not stopped. It has been raining all day and it is **still** raining now.

sting (stinging, stung)

If an insect or a plant **stings** you, a small sharp point goes into your skin and hurts you. Bees and wasps can **sting** you.

stir (stirring, stirred)

When you **stir** something, you move something like a spoon around to mix it.

stole Look at **steal**.

stolen Look at **steal**.

stomach

Your **stomach** is the place inside your body where your food goes after you eat it.

stone

1 A **stone** is a piece of rock.
2 A **stone** is also the hard round thing in the middle of some fruits, like peaches and cherries.

stood Look at **stand**.

stop (stopping, stopped)

1 If you **stop** what you are doing, you do not do it any more. **Stop** talking and listen for a moment.

2 When something that was moving **stops**, it stands still. We **stopped** because some cows were blocking our way.

store (storing, stored)

If you **store** something somewhere, you put it there so that you can use it later. These biscuits will stay fresh for longer if you **store** them in a tin.

storm

A **storm** is very bad weather with strong winds and a lot of rain or snow. Many **storms** also have thunder and lightning.

story (stories)

A **story** tells you about things that happened. Some **stories** are about real things and others are made up. Grandpa read me a **story** about a girl who had lots of exciting adventures.

straight

If something is **straight**, it does not bend, curl or turn to the side. You can use a ruler to draw a **straight** line. Ben's hair is curly but mine is **straight**.

strange

1 Something that is **strange** is very different from what you expect. I am drawing a picture of a **strange** animal. It would be **strange** if you didn't know your own name.
2 A **strange** place is somewhere you have never been to before.

straw

1 **Straw** is the dry stems of plants like wheat. The horse sleeps on **straw** in winter.
2 A **straw** is a long, thin tube made of paper or plastic for drinking through.

Paulo likes drinking through a **straw**.

stream

A **stream** is a small river. The dog is jumping over the **stream**.

street

A **street** is a road in a town, with buildings along each side.

stretch (stretches, stretching, stretched)

If you **stretch** something, you make it longer or wider by pulling it.

strict

If somebody is **strict**, they expect people to do what they say and to obey rules. Our teacher is **strict**, but we like her.

string

1 **String** is very thin rope. You use **string** for tying up things like parcels.
2 Musical instruments like guitars have **strings** that you touch to make sounds.

strip

A **strip** is a long, thin piece of something. We are cutting the paper into **strips**.

stripe

A **stripe** is a coloured line on something.

strong

1 If you are **strong**, you have a lot of power. Are you **strong** enough to lift this heavy box?
2 If something is **strong**, you cannot break it easily.
3 If a taste or smell is **strong**, you can notice it easily. This cheese has a very **strong** smell.

stuck Look at **stick**.

student

A **student** is somebody who is learning something.

stung Look at **sting**.

submarine

A **submarine** is a boat that can travel under water.

subtract

(subtracting, subtracted)

To **subtract** means to take one number away from another. If you **subtract** three from five you are left with two.

suck (sucking, sucked)

When you **suck**, you pull liquid into your mouth from something. The baby is **sucking** milk from a bottle.

sudden

Something that is **sudden** happens quickly and when you do not expect it. There was a **sudden** loud noise.

suddenly

Suddenly means quickly. It was sunny all day and then **suddenly** it started to rain.

sugar

Sugar is something that you put in food and drinks to make them sweet.

suit

A **suit** is a set of clothes that match because they are made out of the same cloth. A **suit** can be a jacket and trousers, or a jacket and a skirt.

sum

When you do a **sum**, you work out something with numbers.

Another word that sounds like **sum** is **some**.

summer

Summer is the hottest part of the year. It comes between the spring and the autumn.

Another word that sounds like **Sun** is **son**.

Sun

The **Sun** is the big, bright star that we can see in the sky during the day. The **Sun** gives us light and keeps us warm.

sung

Look at **sing**.

sunk

Look at **sink**.

sunny (sunnier, sunniest)

When the Sun is shining brightly, it is **sunny**. It's a **sunny** day today.

sunshine

Sunshine is the light and heat from the Sun. My cat likes sitting in the **sunshine**.

supermarket

A **supermarket** is a big shop where you can buy food and other things. You take what you want as you go around and then pay for everything on your way out.

supper

Supper is a meal that people eat in the evening.

sure

If you are **sure**, you know that something is right. I am **sure** I know that boy.

surface

The **surface** of something is the outside part. The **surface** of the road is full of holes.

surprise

A **surprise** is something that happens that you did not expect.

We baked a cake as a **surprise** for my brother's birthday.

swallow (swallowing, swallowed)

When you **swallow** food or drink, it goes down your throat.

swam Look at **swim**.

swan

A **swan** is a big, white bird that lives on water. A young **swan** is called a cygnet.

sweater

A **sweater** is something that covers the top part of your body and your arms to keep you warm. **Sweaters** are often made of wool.

sweep (sweeping, swept)

When you **sweep**, you clean a floor with a brush.

sweet

Sweet foods and drinks have a taste like sugar. Ice cream is **sweet**.

swept Look at **sweep**.

swim (swimming, swam, swum)

When you **swim**, you use your arms and legs to move your body through water. I am going **swimming** this afternoon.

swing

1 (swinging, swung) When something **swings**, it moves backwards and forwards through the air. You **swing** your arms when you walk.
2 A **swing** is a seat for swinging that hangs on two ropes or chains.

switch (switches)

A **switch** is something that you press or turn to stop or start something working. You press this **switch** to turn on the television.

swum Look at **swim**.

swung Look at **swing**.

Some words, such as **cycle**, sound as if they begin with **s**, but you will find them in the dictionary under **c**.

Word play
Can you find the names of nine animals hidden in this box?

b	s	h	e	e	p
a	n	t	o	r	a
t	a	s	w	a	n
o	k	x	l	t	d
z	e	b	r	a	a

Answers on page 176.

table

A **table** is a piece of furniture with legs and a flat top.

> Another word that sounds like **tail** is **tale**.

tail

A **tail** is the part of an animal that grows out of the back end of its body. Aeroplanes also have **tails**.

tale

A **tale** is a story. Do you know the **tale** of Cinderella and the ugly sisters?

> Another word that sounds like **tale** is **tail**.

talk (talking, talked)

When you **talk**, you say words. My little sister can't **talk** yet because she is only a baby.

tall

Somebody or something that is **tall** goes up a long way from the ground. There are a lot of **tall** buildings in the city centre.

tame

A **tame** animal is not wild or afraid of people. Pets are **tame** animals.

tap

A **tap** is something that you turn to make water flow. Baths and sinks have **taps**.

taste

1 (tasting, tasted) When you **taste** food, you put it in your mouth to see what it is like. You **taste** food with your tongue.
2 A **taste** is what food or drink is like in your mouth. I don't like the **taste** of lemons.

taught Look at **teach**.

tea

Tea is a drink that is made by adding boiling water to the dried leaves of the **tea** plant. Would you like a cup of **tea**?

teach (teaches, teaching, taught)

You **teach** somebody by helping them to learn something or by showing them how to do something. My mum is **teaching** me to use a computer.

teacher

A **teacher** is somebody who teaches something, usually in a school. Mrs Smith is our **teacher**.

team

A **team** is a group of people who play a game together on the same side. There are five players in a basketball **team**.

tear *rhymes with *here*

A **tear** is a drop of water that comes from your eye when you cry.

tear *rhymes with *hair*
(tearing, tore, torn)

When you **tear** something, you pull it apart.

Sarah is **tearing** the piece of paper in half.

teeth Look at **tooth**.

telephone

You use a **telephone** for talking to people who are far away. The **telephone** rang but nobody answered it.

telescope

You use a **telescope** for looking at things that are far away and making them look bigger and closer.

television

A **television** is an instrument in the shape of a box with a glass screen. You use a **television** to watch programmes with pictures and sounds. The short word for **television** is **TV**.

tell (telling, told)

If you **tell** somebody about something, you say what you know about it. Please could you **tell** me how to open this box?

tennis

Tennis is a game that two or four people can play. The players hit a ball to each other over a net.

tent

A **tent** is a place to sleep in that is made of cloth and held up by poles and ropes. Some people stay in **tents** when they are on holiday.

term

A **term** is a part of the school year when school is open. The summer **term** starts in April and ends in July.

terrible

Something that is **terrible** is very, very bad. The weather is **terrible** – it has been raining all day.

test

A **test** is a way of finding out how much somebody knows about something. We had a spelling **test** at school today.

theatre

A **theatre** is a place where people go to see plays.

thick

1 Something that is **thick** measures a lot from one side to the other. Castles have very **thick** walls.
2 Liquids that are **thick** do not flow easily. Honey is a **thick** liquid.

thin (thinner, thinnest)

1 If something is **thin**, it is not very far between the two sides. The pages of this dictionary are **thin**.
2 Thin also means not fat.

think (thinking, thought)

When you **think**, you have ideas in your head. **Think** carefully before you answer this question.

third

Third means next after the second one. Gemma came first in the race, Paul came second and I came **third**.

thirsty

When you are **thirsty**, you want something to drink. I was so **thirsty** that I drank three glasses of water.

thought

1 A **thought** is an idea. Have you had any **thoughts** about what you would like to do this afternoon?
2 Look at **think**.

thread

Thread is a very long, thin piece of material like cotton or wool. People use a needle and **thread** to sew.

threw Look at **throw**.

Another word that sounds like **threw** is **through**.

throat

Your **throat** is the part at the back of your mouth. I have got a sore **throat**.

through

Through means from one side to the other. We crawled **through** a hole in the fence.

Another word that sounds like **through** is **threw**.

throw

(throwing, threw, thrown)

When you **throw** something, you make it move through the air using your hand.

Levi has **thrown** the ball into the air.

thumb

Your **thumb** is the short, fat finger on one side of your hand.

thunder

Thunder is the loud noise that you hear in the sky after a flash of lightning. You hear **thunder** when there is a **thunderstorm**.

ticket

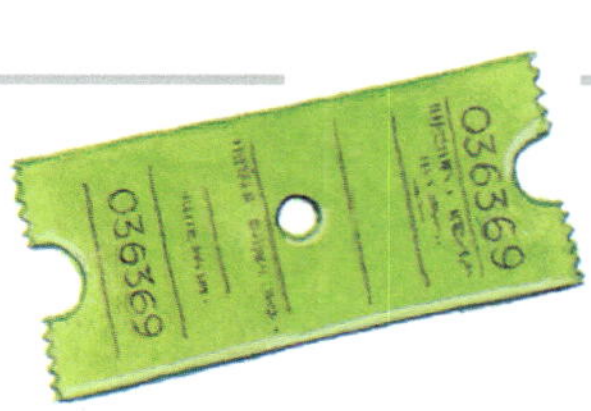

A **ticket** is a small piece of paper that shows that you have paid for something. You have to have a **ticket** to travel by train. My mum bought **tickets** for the film.

tie

1 (tying, tied) When you **tie** something, you hold it together with something like string or ribbon

Alice is **tying** her laces.

2 A **tie** is a long, thin piece of cloth that you can tie around the neck of a shirt so that it hangs down the front.

tiger

A **tiger** is a big, wild cat with orange fur and black stripes. **Tigers** live in Asia.

tight

If something is **tight**, it is not loose or easy to take off. These shoes are too **tight** for me – my feet are hurting.

time

Time is when something happens. We measure **time** in years, months, weeks, days, hours, minutes, and seconds. "What **time** is it?" "It's two o'clock."

tin

1 **Tin** is a kind of metal that is silver in colour.
2 A **tin** is a kind of container. You can buy food like fruit and soup in **tins**.

tiny (tinier, tiniest)

Something that is **tiny** is very small. An ant is a **tiny** animal.

tired

When you are **tired**, you feel that you want to rest or to go to sleep. Mum felt **tired** so she went to bed early.

toad

A **toad** is an animal that looks like a large frog. I saw a **toad** by the pond in our garden.

toe

Your **toes** are the five parts that you have at the end of each foot.

together

Together means with each other. My friend and I always walk to school **together**.

told Look at **tell**.

tomato (tomatoes)

A **tomato** is a soft, round, red fruit that is used to make foods like soup and ketchup.

tongue

Your **tongue** is the long, pink part inside your mouth. Your **tongue** helps you to taste, to swallow food and to speak.

tool

A **tool** is something that we use to help us do work. A hammer is a **tool** that is used for hitting nails into things.

tooth (teeth)

A **tooth** is one of the hard, white parts inside your mouth. We bite and chew food with our **teeth**.

top

1 The **top** of something is the highest part.

The cat climbed to the **top** of the tree.

2 A **top** is something that covers a thing like a bottle or a jar. Don't forget to put the **top** back on the toothpaste tube.

tore Look at **tear**.

torn Look at **tear**.

tortoise

A **tortoise** is an animal with a hard shell on its back. **Tortoises** move slowly. Some people keep them as pets.

touch (touches, touching, touched)

1 If you **touch** something, you put your hand on it and feel it. Don't **touch** the iron – it's very hot!
2 If two things are **touching**, there is no space between them. Jonjo and Felicity sat close together with their backs **touching**.

towards

Towards means in the direction of something. My dog ran **towards** me.

towel

A **towel** is a large piece of cloth you use to dry yourself with.

town

A **town** is a place where there are a lot of streets, houses, shops and other buildings. A **town** is bigger than a village.

toy (toys)

A **toy** is something you can play with. We made the kitten a **toy** out of string.

trace (tracing, traced)

When you **trace** a picture, you put a thin piece of paper over it and then draw over the lines of the picture to copy it.

tractor

A **tractor** is a strong machine with big wheels. Farmers use **tractors** for pulling heavy things.

traffic

Traffic is all the cars, buses, vans and lorries moving along the road. At some times of the day there is a lot of **traffic**.

traffic lights

Traffic lights are a set of red, orange and green lights by the road that tell drivers when to stop and go.

train

1 A **train** is something that you can travel in. It is pulled by an engine along a railway line. **Trains** stop at stations.
2 (training, trained) To **train** a person or an animal is to teach them how to do something. Some dogs have been **trained** to help blind people.

trap

A **trap** is something that is used to catch an animal or a person. They set a **trap** to catch the rat.

travel (travelling, travelled)

When you **travel**, you go from one place to another. We **travelled** to my aunt and uncle's house by train.

treasure

Treasure is a big pile of things like gold, silver and jewels. The pirates hid their **treasure** in a cave.

tree

A **tree** is a plant with branches, leaves and a thick stem, called a trunk, made of wood. Many **trees** can grow to be very tall.

triangle

A **triangle** is a shape with three straight sides.

trick

1 A **trick** is a clever plan to make somebody believe something that is not true. We played a **trick** on our teacher by hiding his books when he wasn't looking.
2 A **trick** is also something that seems impossible. The magician does card **tricks**.

trip

1 A **trip** is when you travel somewhere. We went on a school **trip** to the museum.
2 (tripping, tripped) When you **trip**, you hit your foot against something and fall. Put your toys away before somebody **trips** over them.

trouble

If you have **trouble** doing something, there are problems. The woman in the library had a lot of **trouble** finding the book I wanted.

trousers

Trousers are something that you wear. They cover your legs and bottom.

truck

A **truck** is a lorry. People use **trucks** to carry big, heavy things.

true

1 If something is **true**, it really happened. Is that a **true** story?
2 **True** also means right. It is **true** that the Earth is round.

trumpet

A **trumpet** is a musical instrument that you play by blowing into it.

trunk

1 The **trunk** of a tree is the thick, round part that grows up from the ground. Branches grow from the **trunk**.
2 An elephant's **trunk** is its long nose, which it uses to lift food and water.
3 A **trunk** is also a large box for keeping things in.

trust (trusting, trusted)

If you **trust** somebody, you know they will do what they promise. Mrs Wilson **trusted** Alice to look after the younger children.

truth

The **truth** is what is true. You should always tell the **truth**.

try (tries, trying, tried)

1 When you **try** to do something, you do your best to do it. I **tried** to lift the heavy box, but I couldn't.
2 To **try** also means to do or taste something to see if you like it. Have you **tried** this chocolate drink? It's delicious!

tub

A **tub** is a wide, round container. You can buy ice cream in **tubs**.

tube

A **tube** is a long, hollow thing like a pipe made of plastic, metal, rubber or glass.

tunnel

A **tunnel** is a long hole through a hill or under the ground. The train went through a **tunnel** in the mountains.

turn (turning, turned)

1 When something **turns**, it moves around. The wheels of a bike **turn** when you push the pedals.
2 When something **turns** into another thing, it changes into that thing. Water **turns** into ice when it gets very cold.

twin

Twins are two children who have the same mother and who were born at the same time. A lot of **twins** look alike. David and Richard are **twins**.

twist (twisting, twisted)

If you **twist** something, you turn it around and around. I **twisted** the wires together.

tying Look at **tie**.

tyre

A **tyre** is a circle made of rubber that covers the outside of a wheel. My bike needs a new back **tyre**.

ugly (uglier, ugliest)

Somebody or something that is **ugly** is not nice to look at. Pretend you are a monster and make an **ugly** face.

umbrella

An **umbrella** is a thing that you hold over you to stay dry when it rains. It is made of a round piece of cloth joined to a long handle.

uncle

Your **uncle** is the brother of your father or your mother, or the husband of your aunt.

under

1 Under means lower than the bottom of something. The dog is hiding **under** the chair. **2 Under** also means covered by something. A plant's roots grow **under** the ground.

understand (understanding, understood)

If you **understand** something, you know what it means. Do you **understand** all the words on this page?

undress (undressing, undressed)

When you **undress**, you take off your clothes. You get dressed in the morning and you **undress** at night.

unhappy (unhappier, unhappiest)

If you are **unhappy**, you are sad. Nicky was **unhappy** when her dog ran away.

uniform

A **uniform** is a set of special clothes that people wear to show they belong to the same group. Nurses, the police and people who work in restaurants wear **uniforms**.

universe

The **universe** is the Earth, the Sun, the Moon and all the other planets and stars. The Earth is only a very tiny spot in the **universe**.

until

Until means up to a certain time. I go to school every day from nine o'clock **until** three o'clock.

unusual

Something that is **unusual** is not usual. It is **unusual** to see a cat without a tail.

up

If somebody or something goes **up**, it moves from a lower place to a higher place. It's hard work riding **up** the hill.

upset

When you are **upset**, you feel unhappy. Bobby was **upset** when he lost his balloon.

upside down

If something is **upside down**, the bottom is at the top and the top is at the bottom.

The letter 'u' on Mia's shirt is **upside down**.

upstairs

Upstairs means to a higher part of a building. I am going **upstairs** to bed now.

urgent

If something is **urgent**, it must be done straight away.

use (using, used)

When you **use** something, you do a job with it. You **use** a ruler for measuring and drawing straight lines.

useful

If something is **useful**, it helps you in some way. An umbrella is **useful** when it rains.

usual

Something is **usual** if it happens most of the time. Today I got up at eight o'clock as **usual**.

usually

Usually means almost always. The weather is **usually** cold in winter.

Word play

Copy this list of words onto a piece of paper. Then close your dictionary and see how quickly you can put them in alphabetical order.

usually upset unusual undress understand usual

If the second letter of the words is the same, look at the third letter and so on.

Answers at the back!

valley (valleys)

A **valley** is low land between hills. Many **valleys** have rivers flowing through them.

van

A **van** is a small covered lorry used for carrying things.

vanish (vanishes, vanishing, vanished)

If something **vanishes**, it goes away suddenly. We watched the plane until it **vanished** above the clouds.

vase

A **vase** is something that you fill with water and put flowers in.

vegetable

A **vegetable** is a part of plant that people eat. Carrots and potatoes are **vegetables**.

vet

A **vet** is a kind of doctor who looks after animals that are ill or hurt.

video

A **video** is a special kind of tape which records and stores pictures and sound. You play it on a **video recorder**.

village

A **village** is a small group of houses and other buildings. **Villages** are smaller than towns and they are usually in the country.

violin

A **violin** is a musical instrument made of wood. You hold it under your chin and move a stick called a bow across it to play it.

visit (visiting, visited)

If you **visit** somebody or something, you go to see them. Natasha **visited** her friend who was ill in hospital.

voice

Your **voice** is the sound that you make when you speak or sing. I could hear **voices** outside my room.

Vegetables

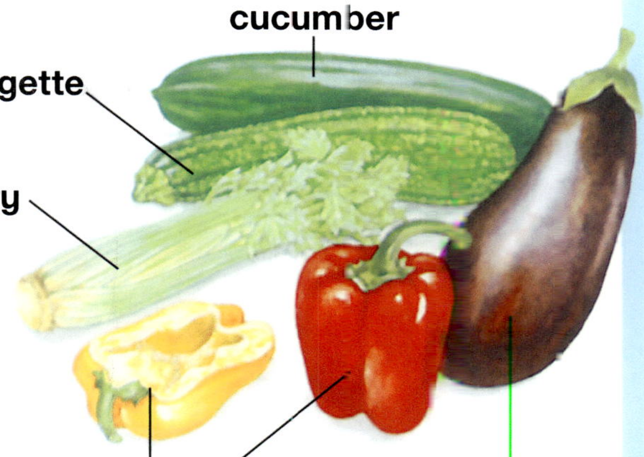

Grow a carrot top
Use a carrot top that still has leaves. Put it in water and look for new roots growing.

wagon

A **wagon** is used to carry people and things from one place to another. It has four wheels and it is usually pulled along by horses.

wait (waiting, waited)

If you **wait**, you stay where you are because you are expecting something to happen.

We **waited** for half an hour before the bus came.

wake (waking, woke, woken)

When you **wake** up, you stop sleeping. Please **wake** me up early tomorrow.

walk (walking, walked)

When you **walk**, you move along on your feet. I **walk** to school every day.

wall

1 A **wall** is one of the sides of a building or of a room. A room usually has four **walls**.
2 A **wall** is also something made of bricks or stones that you can see around some fields and gardens.

Wendy is painting the **wall**.

want (wanting, wanted)

When you **want** something, you would like to have it. Do you **want** a drink?

war

A **war** is a time when armies are fighting against each other.

Another word that sounds like **war** is **wore**.

warm

Warm means quite hot, but not too hot. You wear gloves in winter to keep your hands **warm**.

wash
(washes, washing, washed)

When you **wash** something, you make it clean with soap and water. Remember to **wash** your hands before you eat.

wasp

A **wasp** is a flying insect with yellow and black stripes on its body. **Wasps** can sting.

waste (wasting, wasted)

If you **waste** something, you use more of it than you need. You mustn't **waste** electricity by leaving all the lights on.

watch

1 (watches, watching, watched) If you **watch** something, you look at it for a while. Kim is **watching** television.
2 (watches) A **watch** is a small clock that you wear around your wrist.

water

Water is the clear liquid that is in seas, lakes and rivers. All living things need **water**.

wave

1 A **wave** is a curved line of water moving across a sea.
2 (waving, waved) When you **wave**, you move your hand up and down to say hello or goodbye to somebody.

Jenna is **waving** to her friend.

wax

Wax is used to make candles and crayons. It goes soft and melts when it gets very hot.

way (ways)

1 A **way** of doing something is how you do it. Do it the **way** I showed you.
2 A **way** is also how you get from one place to another.
Can you tell me the **way** to the station, please?

Another word that sounds like **way** is **weigh**.

weak

Somebody or something that is **weak** is not strong. If you didn't eat or drink, you would soon become very **weak**.

Another word that sounds like **weak** is **week**.

wear (wearing, wore, worn)

1 When you **wear** clothes, you have them on your body. Lola is **wearing** a red dress.
2 When something **wears** out, it cannot be used any more.
I played my new game all week and the batteries soon **wore** out.

Another word that sounds like **wear** is **where**.

weather

The **weather** is how hot, cold, windy, rainy or sunny it is outside. What's the **weather** like today? We had bad **weather** on holiday – it rained all the time.

web

A **web** is a kind of net that a spider makes to catch insects to eat.

week

A **week** is seven days. There are 52 **weeks** in a year.

Another word that sounds like **week** is **weak**.

weigh (weighing, weighed)

You **weigh** something on scales to find out how heavy it is. Mia is **weighing** some bananas.

Another word that sounds like **weigh** is **way**.

well (better, best)

1 When you do something **well**, you do it in a good way. Paul plays the flute very **well**.
2 If you are **well**, you are healthy. I don't feel very **well** today.

west

The **west** is where the Sun goes down in the evening. The opposite direction is east.

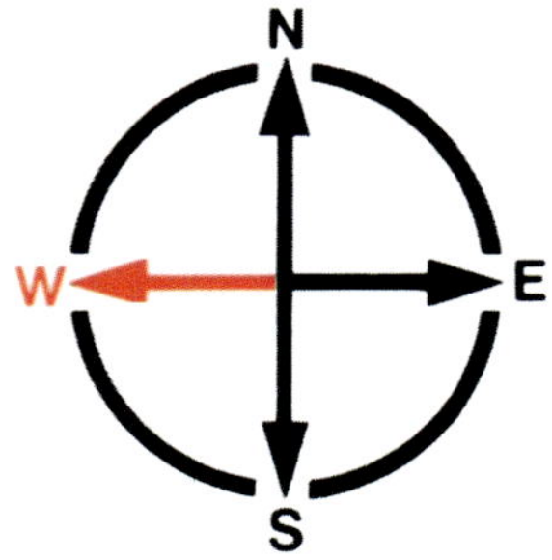

wet (wetter, wettest)

Something that is **wet** is covered with water or full of water. You will get **wet** if you go out in the rain.

whale

A **whale** is a very large animal that lives in the sea. **Whales** look like fish but they are really mammals.

wheat

Wheat is a plant that farmers grow. We use its seeds, called grain, to make flour.

wheel

A **wheel** is a round thing. **Wheels** go round and round to move things along the ground. Cars, lorries and wheelchairs have **wheels**.

whisper (whispering, whispered)

When you **whisper**, you speak very quietly. You **whisper** to somebody when you don't want other people to hear you.

whistle

1 (whistling, whistled) When you **whistle**, you make a musical sound by blowing air through your lips. I **whistled** to my dog to make him come back.

2 A **whistle** is a small instrument which makes a sound when you blow through it.

whole

The **whole** of something is all of it. Wilf ate the **whole** cake – he didn't leave any.

Another word that sounds like **whole** is **hole**.

wide

Something that is **wide** measures a lot from one side to the other. A motorway is a very **wide** kind of road.

wife (wives)

A man's **wife** is the woman he is married to.

wild

Wild animals and plants are animals and plants that are not looked after by people. Squirrels are **wild** animals.

win (winning, won)

When you **win** a game or a race, you finish first or do better than everybody else. I **won** the 100-metre race.

wind

The **wind** is air that is moving very fast. The **wind** blew the man's hat off.

window

A **window** is a hole in the wall of a building that lets in light from outside. **Windows** usually have glass in them.

wing

Birds, bats and some insects have **wings** which they use to fly. Aeroplanes also have **wings**.

winter

Winter is the coldest part of the year. **Winter** comes after autumn and before spring.

wire

A **wire** is a long, thin piece of metal that bends easily. Electricity goes along **wires**.

wish (wishes, wishing, wished)

If you **wish** for something, you want to have it or you want it to happen very much. I **wish** I could fly.

witch
(witches)

A **witch** is a woman who has magic powers.

Another word that sounds like **witch** is **which**.

wives
Look at **wife**.

wizard
A **wizard** is a man who has magic powers. The **wizard** is wearing a tall, pointed hat.

woke
Look at **wake**.

woken
Look at **wake**.

wolf
(wolves)

A **wolf** is a wild animal that looks like a big dog, with a pointed nose and pointed ears. A young **wolf** is called a cub.

woman
(women)

A **woman** is a grown-up female person.

won
Look at **win**.

Another word that sounds like **won** is **one**.

wonder
(wondering, wondered)

If you **wonder** about something, you think about something that you do not know the answer to. I **wonder** why the Earth is round.

wonderful
If something is **wonderful**, it is very good. I like your picture. I think it's **wonderful**.

wood
1 Wood is what trees are made of. People use **wood** to make things like tables and chairs.
2 A **wood** is a place where there are a lot of trees growing near each other. We went for a walk in the **wood**.

Another word that sounds like **wood** is **would**.

wool
Wool is the soft, thick hair that grows on sheep. **Wool** is used for making cloth and for knitting. Jumpers and scarves are often made of **wool**.

word
We use **words** when we speak or write. **Words** are made of letters of the alphabet and each word means something.

wore
Look at **wear**.

Another word that sounds like **wore** is **war**.

work
1 Work is what somebody does as a job, or something else that they have to do. What time does your mum go to **work**?
2 (working, worked) When you **work**, you do or make something. Helen **works** in a bank.
3 If a machine **works**, it does what it should do. This clock doesn't **work** any more.

world
The **world** is the planet that we live on, and all its countries and people. Which is the biggest city in the **world**?

worm
A **worm** is a small creature with a long, thin body and no legs. Many **worms** live in the ground.

worn
Look at **wear**.

worry
(worries, worrying, worried)

If you **worry**, you keep thinking of bad things that might happen. Mum **worries** when I'm late coming home from school.

worse
Worse means more bad. The weather was bad yesterday, but it's **worse** today.

worst
Worst means most bad. Can you remember the **worst** food you have ever eaten?

wrap
(wrapping, wrapped)

If you **wrap** something, you cover it with something else.

wrist
Your **wrist** is the thin part of your arm just above your hand.

write
(writing, wrote, written)

When you **write**, you make words with a pen or pencil. Milo is **writing** with his new pen.

Another word that sounds like **write** is **right**.

wrong
Wrong means not right or not good. It's **wrong** to say that six and two make nine. Stealing money is also **wrong**.

wrote
Look at **write**.

a b c d e f g h i j k l m n o p q r s t u v **w** x y z

X-ray

An **X-ray** is a special kind of photograph that shows what the inside of your body looks like. At the hospital the doctor showed me an **X-ray** of my chest.

xylophone *say *zylofone*

A **xylophone** is a musical instrument that is made of flat bars of different lengths. You play it by hitting these bars with small hammers to make music.

Word play

Do you know what the young of these animals are called? The dictionary explanations will help you.

goose

gosling

sheep

horse

wolf

Answers on page 176.

yacht *rhymes with *got*

A **yacht** is a boat with sails or an engine. Some **yachts** are used for racing. Last week my brother and I went sailing with my uncle on his **yacht**.

yawn (yawning, yawned)

When you **yawn**, you open your mouth wide and breathe deeply. People **yawn** when they are tired.

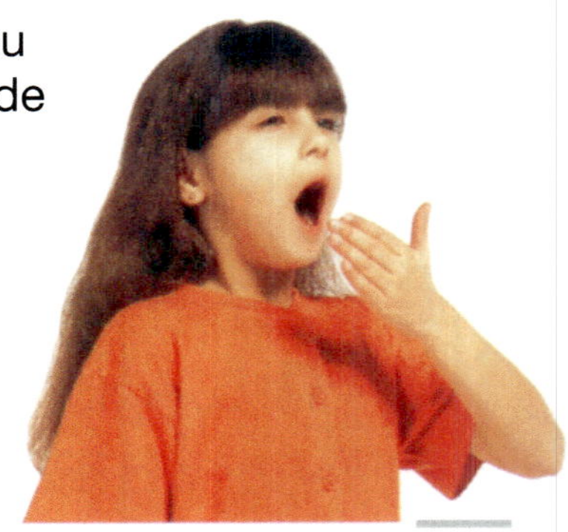

Rosa is **yawning**.

year

A **year** is an amount of time. There are 12 months in one **year**.

yell (yelling, yelled)

If you **yell**, you shout. "Come over here!" she **yelled**.

yesterday

Yesterday means the day before today. Today is Tuesday, so **yesterday** was Monday.

yolk *say *yoke*

A **yolk** is the yellow part in the middle of an egg.

young

A person or an animal that is **young** has not been alive for very long. Puppies are **young** dogs, and lambs are **young** sheep.

zebra

A **zebra** is an animal like a horse with black and white stripes on its body. **Zebras** live in Africa.

zero (zeros)

Zero is the number 0. You write ten with a one and a **zero**.

zigzag

A **zigzag** is a line that bends sharply up and down.

zip

A **zip** is a long metal or plastic thing that holds together two edges of material. Trousers and bags often have **zips**.

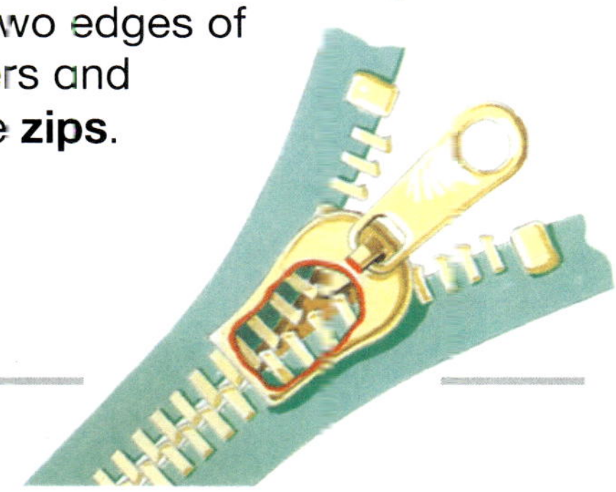

zoo

A **zoo** is a place where wild animals are kept so that people can go to look at them.

Other useful words

Days

Monday
Tuesday
Wednesday
Thursday
Friday
Saturday
Sunday

Months

January
February
March
April
May
June
July
August
September
October
November
December

Numbers

1 one
2 two
3 three
4 four
5 five
6 six
7 seven
8 eight
9 nine
10 ten
11 eleven
12 twelve
13 thirteen
14 fourteen
15 fifteen
16 sixteen
17 seventeen
18 eighteen
19 nineteen
20 twenty
21 twenty-one
30 thirty
40 forty
50 fifty
60 sixty
70 seventy
80 eighty
90 ninety
100 a hundred
101 a hundred and one
1,000 a thousand
1,000,000 a million

Measurements

1 centimetre = 10 millimetres
1 metre = 100 centimetres
1 kilometre = 1,000 metres

1 gram = 1,000 milligrams
1 kilogram = 100 grams

1 litre = 1,000 millilitres

Telling the time

It's two o'clock.

It's ten past six.

It's quarter past seven.

It's half past four.

It's quarter to eleven.

Spellchecker

Words we often use

about
against
ago
already
also
am
and
any
anybody
anyone
anything
anyway
anywhere
are
aren't = are not
as
at
away

be
became
because
become
becoming
been
being
but
by

came
can
cannot = can not
can't = can not
come
coming
could
couldn't = could not

did
didn't = did not
do
does
doesn't = does not
doing
done
don't

either
else
ever
every
everybody
everyone

few
for
from

get
getting
go
goes
going
gone
got

had
happen
happened
happening
has
have
haven't = have not
having
her
here
he's = he is
him
his
how

I'd = I would or I had
if
I'll = I will or I shall
I'm = I am
in
into
is
isn't = is not
its
it's = it is
I've = I have

just

least
less
let's = let us
letting
lot

made
make
many
may
me
might
mine
more
most
much
must
mustn't = must not
my
myself

neither
nobody
none
no one
not
nothing
now
nowhere

of
off
OK
on
once
onto
or
other
our
out

perhaps
probably
put
putting

shall
should
shouldn't = should not
so
some
somebody
someone
something
sometimes
somewhere
still
such

take
taken
taking
than
that
their
them
then
there
these
they
they're = they are
this
those
till
to
today
tomorrow
tonight
too
took

until
up
upon
us

very

was
wasn't = was not
we
well
we'll = we will
went
were
weren't = were not
what
when
where
which
who
whose
why
will
with
would
wouldn't = would not

yet
your
you're = you are
you've = you have

World play answers

Page 92
live (it becomes 'evil' when you spell it backwards). The other words are: wolf (flow), net (ten), pot (top).
Did you think of any more?

Page 99
If you hold the message up to a mirror, you should be able to read:

What
keys are
furry?
Monkeys!

Page 105

				1 n	i	2 n	e
				o		a	
				s		i	
		3 n	e	e	d	l	e
		e					
		s					
4 n	o	t	e				

Page 117
bread, pizza, potato, cheese

Page 128
tail/tale
way/weigh
hole/whole
dear/deer
plane/plain

Page 132
sandwich (sand + witch!)
butterfly (butter + fly)
rainbow (rain + bow)
lighthouse (light + house)

Page 146
balloon, scissors, pencil, giraffe, iron

Page 153
sheep, ant, swan, zebra, bat, snae, owl, rat, panda

Page 163
understand, undress, unusual, upset, usual, usually

Page 172
goose/gosling
sheep/lamb
horse/foal
wolf/cub